PENGUIN BOOKS

THREADING WORLDS: CONVERSATIONS ON MENTAL HEALTH

GROWING PAINS

As an internationally recognized spiritual teacher, professional artist, social healer, life coach, and community leader, Hun Ming Kwang is relentless in his mission to illuminate individuals to their deepest truths, callings and authentic selves, helping them awaken and harness their power to actualize their lives at their highest creative potential. Today, he has helped over 10,000 individuals transform their lives and attain a higher level of awareness.

He also focuses on championing humanitarian campaigns and efforts to invoke and inspire awareness on social causes such as mental health and suicide prevention at a national level. He is the founder and co-artistic director of ThisConnect.today, where he designs and produces experiential art, interactive films and conscious conversations to make a difference to the public.

OTHER BOOKS IN THE SERIES

Stories We Don't Tell, Penguin Random House SEA, 2022
Weaving between Light and Shadows, Said and Unsaid,
Penguin Random House SEA, 2022
Singapore and Mental Health, Penguin Random House SEA, 2022

Threading Worlds: Conversations on Mental Health
Growing Pains

Hun Ming Kwang

PENGUIN BOOKS

An imprint of Penguin Random House

PENGUIN BOOKS

USA | Canada | UK | Ireland | Australia
New Zealand | India | South Africa | China | Southeast Asia

Penguin Books is part of the Penguin Random House group of companies whose addresses can be found at global.penguinrandomhouse.com

Published by Penguin Random House SEA Pvt. Ltd
9, Changi South Street 3, Level 08-01,
Singapore 486361

First published in Penguin Books by Penguin Random House SEA 2022

10 9 8 7 6 5 4 3 2 1

ISBN 9789815058253

Typeset in Garamond by MAP Systems, Bengaluru, India

www.penguin.sg

Contents

Foreword

The latest Singapore Mental Health Study shows one in seven people has experienced some mental health challenges in their lifetime and more than 75 per cent of these did not seek any professional help.[1] *Threading Worlds: Conversations on Mental Health* Volumes seek to close this treatment gap.

The transcribed authentic voices of healthcare professionals and other community leaders and those with lived experiences will help us reach the self-realization of our own state of mental wellness. It will move us to co-create a safe space for the community to talk openly about the challenges and the solutions with courage and empathy.

One of the causes of the treatment gap is the stigmatization of the condition driving us from seeking treatment. I have been to ThisConnect's multimedia art exhibitions and one of the works, 'Connection without Sight', shows us how we can connect deeply through our primal senses and emotional centres without succumbing to the superficial judgement of sight.

[1] Subramaniam, M., E. Abdin, J. A. Vaingankar, S. Shafie, B. Y. Chua, R. Sambasivam, Y. J. Zhang, et al., 'Tracking the Mental Health of a Nation: Prevalence and Correlates of Mental Disorders in the Second Singapore Mental Health Study', Epidemiology and Psychiatric Sciences 29, 2020: e29. doi:10.1017/S2045796019000179

Active listening is essential for deep understanding with empathy without which the advice we give and receive are likely to be irrelevant and superfluous. Another work, 'I Feel You', will enable us to stand in the shoes of others and be there to hold that safe, sacred space for another human being.

Masks of Singapore, a six-month local community self-awareness mask-making project, depict the façade that most people portray to one another in our daily interactions. We wear these 'masks' to suppress our true mental state. The making of masks will help us discover our true self and give ourselves permission to express our truth more freely than ever.

This project is a cool way to create a healing place for us to courageously confront our own mental health challenges in a safe space. Wherever these books are found, a safe space to mine the comprehensive information leading one to seek treatment is created. I wish Ming Kwang and his team luck and may their endeavours be perfectly accomplished.

Dr William Wan, PhD, JP
General Secretary,
Singapore Kindness Movement

To You: A Message From The Author

Dear Reader,

If by a stroke of luck, a gesture of goodwill, something about this book resonated with you, it found its way to you, and landed in your hands—let it be a sign that there are certain answers in your life that you're searching for.

Before we begin, I would like to invite you to take a moment to picture this:

You're a student in your teens or early twenties. You're spending thousands of dollars on a formal education as you work your way up to a university degree, studying subjects only for the purpose of excelling in the exams, while juggling several other commitments such as an internship, a part-time job, an extra-curricular activity, to boost your credentials and show your potential employers that you have some degree of holistic development, real-world experience, and a life outside of your studies. Along the way, you might have countless nights of overwhelming stress, pressure, burnout, and negative downward spirals. You ask yourself endlessly: are you disappointing your family? Are you failing the expectations that others have of you? Are you on track to landing a stable job once you graduate? Do you have enough commitments on your plate to ensure you're not any less ambitious than your peers? Your teachers might have good intentions, but the most they tell you is 'Don't stress too much, just remain calm, be positive, be happy, and do your best'—as if those things never automatically occurred to you before. In a world full of adults who appear to have figured out all the answers to life, are you a failure if you can't be positive and calm without distracting yourself and numbing away your anger, sadness, and negativity?

This might also be the period where you struggle to make sense and find your place in your social world. How do people view you? Who are the friends who are going to stick by you as you enter adulthood and into the working world? Who are the people you need to be networking with so that you can position yourself favourably? If you don't manage to find a life partner now, will you still have the time and opportunities to do so once the rat race begins? Are you considered a failure if you never end up settling down with a partner and starting a family?

Or, perhaps you're a corporate executive or a full-time employee in your mid-twenties to thirties, working your daily nine-to-five job. When you first started out, you might have felt excited and driven to finally leave your mark on the world and fulfil your ambitions. But a couple of years later, your life has been entirely segmented into three parts: your day job, the couple of hours at night you have to rest before the next day, and the weekend, where you attempt to make up for all the rest, recreational activities, or social needs that you missed out during the week. Your job pays the bills, but it becomes a mechanical task for you to get through every day. It might not necessarily challenge you to grow as a person. It might not fulfil you, or it might not even be something in your interest in the first place—but you had no choice but to take it on anyway because the job market was bad, there was pressure on you to be doing something great with your life as a culmination of everything you've learnt after you graduated, and you spent nearly twenty years of your life studying and working relentlessly for a paper degree that only serves to tell your potential employers that you're knowledgeable and a specialist in that particular field of study. Surely you've got to work a job that justifies the amount of money, time, blood, sweat, and tears spent on your formal education at the expense of other pursuits that might be less lucrative, but more fulfilling! Otherwise, what did you give up your dreams for? And the unfortunate thing is, perhaps by the fifth year of your career, you're wondering if it is time to switch jobs or try your hands at something new. And for a while, it does bring a breath of fresh air into your life, but after a period of time, you find yourself back at the same spot again—stuck in an endless loop.

Perhaps you're a fifty-something veteran in your field, and you're looking for change, because you've gotten what you wanted out of your career and realized that there's something more you want out of your life. Perhaps you've realized that you neglected every other aspect of your life apart from your career, and you want to rectify that. Perhaps you're a seventy-something retiree, and you're wondering what else there is to life besides living it day by day as you wait for the day you die.

When you encounter such instances, when you question where your life is at, where it is going, what really matters to you, and what your purpose in life really is at the end of the day, I would like to assure you that it's a step you have taken towards looking inwards at yourself. And as much pain and struggle or joy and happiness as it may bring, **keep going**.

Sometimes, we give up our dreams and settle for less while telling ourselves that what we have is good enough. Sometimes, unfortunate circumstances happen to us and make us give up parts of ourselves. Sometimes, the life that we live does not belong to us, but to the expectations of us, to the intentions of others, and to the popular dreams that are trendy at the moment. We gather these second-hand dreams and ideas that belong to others and try to cobble together what our lives could be and what we desire. Be that as it may the answers don't lie there, but within us. However well and good our intentions are, in chasing after the lives of others, we reject and deny what is fundamentally at the root of ourselves: *ourselves.*

The term 'mental health' has rapidly gained traction over the last couple of years, especially in the wake of the pandemic, but there is still a large lack of understanding that mental health is a spectrum in which everyone has their own place depending on where they are in their journey. Some of us are battling mental health conditions and illnesses. Some of us are in the middle, where what we're going through is not necessarily deemed severe enough to be classified as an illness or disorder, but we feel the brunt of our symptoms nonetheless in our everyday lives, and it hinders us from thriving and performing at our optimum capabilities when we need to. Some of us are doing relatively well holistically in the different aspects of our lives, and we're looking at how to take it to the next level. Yet, as I say this, I want to emphasize that somebody who is thriving in their lives can absolutely still go through mental health struggles that are specific to their life's circumstances. Likewise, people who struggle chronically with mental illnesses or disorders can absolutely have days where they're feeling good. Essentially, everybody has mental health, and we relate to it in ways that are entirely unique to our circumstances, our psyche, and our history.

Where you fall on the spectrum is entirely unique to you, and that is why resolving your issues is not a matter of looking outwards at what people have done to resolve their issues and replicating that—although that can certainly give you more data and clarity on what works and what doesn't—but more importantly about looking inwards, understanding the true nature of the issue (since our external reality is really nothing more than a reflection of who we are inside), and examining the core of who *you* are, so that you can do what *you* need to do to triumph over *your* challenges and live *your* **best** life.

Presently, the world is going through a mental health epidemic. More than ever, people are experiencing increasingly severe bouts of depression, anxiety, and on the most severe end of the spectrum, suicidal thoughts, suicide attempts, and suicide cases. In fact, I want to highlight this particular incident that stands out to me. In 2021, a sixteen-year-old student from River Valley High School in Singapore was charged with the murder of a thirteen-year-old schoolmate. Our hearts sank when the news was publicly released. He was found to have been previously assessed at the Institute of Mental Health (IMH) in 2019 after attempting suicide. I believe that this incident highlights the state that children and younger folk are in these days in terms of their mental health and overall wellbeing. There is much more to be done and ground to be covered as this incident happened despite the increase of mental health and wellness programmes in schools and workplaces.

It is precisely because of this that we need to tackle the whole issue of mental health not by adopting a blanket one-size-fits-all solution, but by looking inwards, because suicide never happens in a moment. It never ever does. There are a million moments leading up to that point. Each moment we choose not to face and deal with questions that matter to or bother us, emotions that are 'unpleasant', or conflicts and baggage in our lives, we risk falling or spiralling further down the spectrum. Our issues never really go away until we deal with them and resolve them at the root level head on.

Our life begins the moment we're born—especially in the moments we can no longer consciously remember. The very first time you opened your mouth and cried out loud as a baby, what were your parents' reactions? What was *your* response to that?

The very first time you displayed any bout of anger or rebellion, what were the reactions of the people around you? Did they talk down to you and reprimand you? Did your parents tell you that a good son or daughter would never have exhibited such behaviours? Were you present to the anger and the subtle shame and guilt that ran inside your programming? What did you learn about your emotions, social behaviours, and boundaries consequently from those incidents? The very first time you cried and wished you had your parents' approval and attention but was left waiting and wanting, what was *your* response to that? What did *you* tell yourself about love and relationships?

The very first time you opened up to a teacher or a family member about your dreams to be an artist, a singer, an astronaut, a designer, what was their response? What was *your* response as a reaction to that? What did *you* tell yourself about dreams and reality? What were *your* notions and beliefs around success?

Perhaps, this is about your identity. The very first time you realized that you fell somewhere on the LGBTQ spectrum, and you didn't exactly turn out exactly the way your parents or society expected you to be—'normal' —and you chose courage, came out to these people, but were rejected, or the first time you witnessed someone else in a similar boat get rejected and judged by others, what did it teach *you* about family? What did *you* tell yourself about *your* identity? What did *you* tell yourself about courage, and how did it shape your relationship with it?

One of the most common myths we have around pain is that time heals all wounds, but that couldn't be further from the truth. Time makes us forget that those wounds exist in the first place—it gives us the opportunity to evade or numb ourselves with drugs, alcohol, entertainment, or some other form of escapism from our pain, until we forget about them. And sometimes we go into a delusion thinking that these issues are no more. Silly us.

It doesn't matter what the topic is—the very first statements we tell ourselves about that topic, grows with us as we grow as people throughout the various stages of our lives, and they get reinforced over time as we encounter similar incidents repeatedly. And oftentimes, while these statements may have served and saved us from pain once upon a time in the very first moment, they tend to do us more harm than good in the long run. For instance, if you've always been told that crying is bad and you were punished for it, you might have resorted to numbing away any nuance of sadness or grief the moment you feel it. Doing that might have saved you punishment from your parents while growing up, but as an adult, that numbing has its own repercussions. You might become so numb and disconnected from yourself that you can't tell what matters to you anymore, and you're always looking outwards for answers. Each time you suppress an emotion just adds another drop into the pressure cooker of emotions inside you that's bubbling and waiting to explode when you least expect it, and when you're least prepared to deal with it.

Emotions have always been a tricky topic that we've not yet managed to successfully incorporate well into our upbringing at home and in the education system. Our understanding of emotions is largely limited to happiness, anger, and sadness, but what about everything else in between? What about the subtle emotions like guilt, jealousy, shame, disgust, contempt, or envy? Not to point fingers at anyone in particular, as most parents and educators are only teaching what they've been taught and what they know, and we simply do not know any better, but some of the most unhelpful advice given to kids in school regarding emotions is to just 'not be sad because it doesn't help' and 'be positive and things will work out'. What we've gotten out of that advice are generations of people who are completely out of touch with their emotions, particularly those that are deemed as 'difficult and unpleasant', and are going through the motions of their lives without ever fully participating, engaging, and involving *themselves* in how it unfolds. This only serves to worsen the mental health struggles we face and potentially turn them into long-term mental health disorders.

The unconventional wisdom is to be able to receive the pain such that the pain completes its course. And when the pain no longer has a reason to make you suffer, then perhaps it's time for you to heal. And if you are not busy dying, maybe you will expend some energy into what it takes to live. And if you live, the next question is, how alive do you want to be?

It is crucial to understand that having the ability to manage our emotions is tantamount to managing ourselves as people who are functional and able to contribute value meaningfully to society. It is integral to be able to deal with crisis situations, to being able to lead and work with a team of people from all walks of life with various personalities. It is necessary to be able to connect with another person on a deeper level and hear the things that are left unsaid. It is absolutely paramount to maintaining a healthy overall wellbeing, because a heavy suppression of our emotions eventually leads to the damage on our physical body that manifests as various forms of diseases and illnesses.

The repercussions and consequences of not being able to deal with crisis, of not being able to deal with people both in our personal and professional lives, of having our emotional baggage manifest itself as physical diseases such as cancers, diabetes, or even autoimmune diseases can leave a deep negative impact that takes us years to recover from. Some people never really quite recover. Some resign to the fact that their life is filled with woes so much so that they have accepted that this is where and how their lives end, and these are the people who unfortunately never come to the awareness that there is a way out.

I want to say this: **There is always a way out, no matter how bad circumstances present themselves to you**.

Fortunately, if you're finding *yourself* and looking for *your* place in this world, there is a way—your mental and emotional health is a starting point from which you can begin looking into your psyche, your past, your present, how your future will play out, and what you can do NOW to shape them—just as you shape your life, your paths, and your destinies.

Threading Worlds: Conversations on Mental Health is a literary compilation of conversations my team and I had with seventy-five other contributors in Singapore from March 2021 to May 2021 around the topic of mental health and emotional wellness. These seventy-five contributors come from all walks of life—doctors, nurses, caregivers, counsellors, psychiatrists, therapists, policymakers, social workers, politicians, business leaders, coaches, and youths—and we had facilitated conversations with them on their perspectives on the mental health scene, their own personal journeys, as well as what needs to be done at an individual, community, and national level so that we can move forward and evolve as a collective. Each conversation was transcribed word-for-word with minimized filters deliberately to retain the essence of each conversation such that readers are able to immerse themselves in the conversation and experience it as though they were present in the very moment when the conversation first took place.

This book is intended to serve as a mental and emotional health literacy resource worldwide, and especially in countries like Japan, Korea, and Thailand, where suicide rates are the highest, and the third-world countries where looking inwards and the whole idea of mental health is a luxury in relation to the survivalist fights they have to battle each day instead. Through the perspectives from different walks of life, stories of vulnerability and journeys of recovering and rediscovering oneself, instead of telling people what mental health is and what it is not, we aim to create an immersive experience that allows you to connect to yourself and derive the personal wisdoms and lessons embedded within these stories with your inner-knowing that you can apply to your life. It is best experienced in a distraction-free state when you are able to be *fully and wholly present to yourself* as you experience the book.

As much as you are able to at this moment in your life, I would like to invite you to begin approaching this not exclusively as a mental-health-specific topic, but as a journey of illumination that you embark on to seek the important answers to the questions you have about yourself, your life, and the world around you, so that you can find your footing and live a life that truly matters to you at the end of the day. Many of us, at some point in our lives, ask the bigger questions with heavier weights: Who am I? Where did I come from? What am I meant to do? What is my purpose? What is my truest self? What is the meaning of life itself? And what about my life? How do I live a worthwhile life?

That is right. This has always been about your life, not just your mental health. When we run so hard trying to find our way out of the overwhelming barrage of circumstances our lives are presented with, we might find ourselves reaching our breaking point and collapsing physically, mentally, emotionally, even spiritually. At times when we are defeated, there is no way upwards but to muster every drop of willpower in us to crawl our way to the door and roll ourselves out.

We live in a world where our actions create a ripple effect down the road. Consequently, there are the forces of cause and effect in play. What matters is not what happens in the past or the future, but what you choose to do right now that consequently affects the trajectory of your life. Every passing moment is a second chance to turn it all around. As the saying goes: 'It is easier to build strong children than to repair broken men.' For us to nurture a generation free from the weight of the pain that we and our ancestors bear, we must first heal ourselves to break out of the chains that bind us. To find ourselves, we must first have the courage to give up what we believe is the truth about ourselves and walk the path of self-discovery. Only then do we know what it takes to make a difference to ourselves, and can we have the power to teach others what it means to be a human being in their own right, and be that beacon of light to those finding their way out of the dark.

Ultimately, my goal is to see a society where people thrive, not just survive, and are empowered to be bold, be free, and be ourselves. To have a conscious connection, not just with another person, but with ourselves. To embark on a journey to seek the answers we're searching for. To dare to dream, and dare to make those dreams happen. To gather our courage and take leaps of faith, even if we don't know where and how we'll land. To confront our deepest fears. To stand on the roof and declare our deepest truths to the world. To strike a pose and shout out to the universe, 'This is Me!' To challenge our adversities. To fail in our quest to live a good and fulfilling life, because it is through those failures that we learn what it means to stand for something that matters to us, time and time again, against all odds. To feel deeply, love deeply, and know that there is absolutely no shame in expressing ourselves authentically, no matter what people think.

One life saved can save many other lives. When we embark on the journey of living a life that truly matters to us, we also empower ourselves to step onto a path that enables us to touch another person's life with our highest being. A path along which we create a future that we're excited to step into, a path where we *leave our mark* on the world—so that when the time comes for us to go, we will go not with regrets, but with the knowledge that we have given every drop of our tears, sweat, and blood to living a life true to ourselves.

All of us are a walking morass of questions, on the journey of seeking the answers to living fully alive, and enjoying the ride along the way. Again, to reiterate what I said in the beginning—if by the stroke of luck, a gesture of goodwill, something about this book resonated with you, found its way to you, and landed in your hands—let it be a sign that there are certain answers in your life that you're searching for, and may this book contain some of the lessons and wisdom that can empower you on this journey. When you are done, pass it to another person to pay it forward. Because you never know who may need just that ounce of light to get themselves back on track, since we have adapted to become experts in masking our emotions (I say this sarcastically . . . but this is a very real issue today).

I share this message from a space of love and courage, as somebody who has taken a stand for the transformation of ourselves, transcendence of our limitations, and actualization of our innate potential. And when the time comes, I look forward to meeting you, the reader of this book, someday—the parts of you that can be a beacon of light to the higher consciousness of this world. May our stories, journeys, and collective wisdoms and transformations inspire even more people to begin looking into themselves so that they can begin their own journey of transformation, so that they live their marks on this world, so that when the time comes for us to go, we will go not with regrets, but with the spirit of the life that we've lived well with dignity.

Hun Ming Kwang

Founder, Creative Director, Author of ThisConnect.today

CHAPTER 1

I Want To Give People What I Felt I Never Got

By Desmond Soh, Clinical Psychologist, Annabelle Psychology

Desmond suffered from a suicidal episode when he was twelve years old. After performing poorly during his PSLE, he contemplated suicide because of how difficult it was to deal with the aftermath. As he grew up, he developed an interest in psychology, and on hindsight realized that he wanted to use his experience to help others avoid the unnecessary pain he walked through and give people what he felt he did not receive in the past.

CONNECTING THE DOTS BACKWARDS

MK

Tell me more about yourself.

Desmond

My name is Desmond. I'm one of the clinical psychologists working at Annabelle Psychology (ASPY). I recently received my qualifications in June 2020, because you need to have a master's degree in order to work as a Clinical Psychologist in Singapore. So I've done my training for two years and have been with APSY for the past year. But my involvement in the psychology field dates back to when I was fifteen. I was quite set on becoming a psychologist in secondary school, so I started working with people with special needs. I later did my bachelor's in the US and I worked at a psychiatric hospital in Boston for about a year. I also had a short stint in Hong Kong where I worked with underprivileged children. When I came back to Singapore, I worked at the Institute of Mental Health and a destitute home. Then I got my qualifications, and here I am! I've been working officially as a therapist for two and a half years, but I was already involved in the field before that.

MK

Was there a reason why you wanted to go into the mental health field?

Desmond

There is, actually. I was suicidal when I was in primary six.

It was mainly due to the pressure from academics, pressure from my parents, and the pressure from feeling that I wasn't good enough. I did really badly for PSLE[2] and the aftermath of that was

[2] PSLE: Primary School Leaving Examination

quite difficult to deal with. I was contemplating suicide at that point. I went up to the top floor of my condominium, but I decided not to do it, for reasons that escape me now.

As I was growing up, I didn't give much thought to that suicidal episode. I went through puberty, went through life, and became very interested in psychology even though I never understood why. I just thought it was because it was interesting to know how people think, behave and make meaning in their lives. It wasn't until the past couple of years, because it is highly recommended for psychologists to seek therapy themselves, that I realized why I'm doing what I'm doing. As part of the training to be a psychologist, it's a good idea to see a therapist, because if you don't go for therapy, you don't know how to give therapy. So the process of going through my training made me realize that I wanted to help people not feel the way I did and give people what I felt like I never got at that point in time.

This is my personal journey. I think this is what grounds me as a psychologist. I'm still very early in my career and constantly learning, running into mistakes, moving forward from them, and that's how I got here today.

LOOKING FOR A WAY TO NOT SUFFER

MK

How is it like working with people on the ground? You've worked with diverse communities from around the world, so the world you've seen is a little different. Tell me more about that.

Desmond

When I was in the US, things were a little bit different because the people were really unwell at the hospital I was working at. The job I was doing was a lot more difficult. But at the same time, it's also in an environment like that when I see and hear people talk about their lives, the things they've gone through, the circumstances that I feel we don't hear much in Singapore. Many of the people there came from difficult backgrounds. Some of them went to war and came back with their lives completely changed. Some of them were abandoned by their family because of a mental illness. Some of them were homeless for many years.

Despite the struggles they were going through, there were moments when I felt quite humbled by them. Regardless of the situations they were in, all of them were looking for a way to live a life that would mean something to them. This was also something that I felt is universal, in some ways. Many of the people that I see here as well, despite the families they come from and the situations they're in, are looking for a way out, looking for a way to not suffer. So hearing things like 'it's just a phase, get over it', sometimes rubs me the wrong way because there's so much more than that meets the eye. It feels like what you're insinuating is that the person's not resilient, not mentally strong, that they don't have ability, they're pampered.

MK

All these labels . . .

Desmond

All these labels! Label after label after label. It's not exactly the best description of what is actually happening. Honestly, if I were in the same situations as the people I see, I'm not sure I would be any different. If I was born with certain biological vulnerabilities, if I was born in a certain kind of family, if I grew up in a certain kind of environment, I'm not sure I would be any different.

And so it's precisely the people that I see that have demonstrated mental resilience. They are the ones that demonstrate what it means to suffer, and yet still find a way to continue moving forward. And honestly if that's not mental strength, I don't know what else is. So all these labels really miss the point.

THE SINGAPOREAN DREAM

MK

Amazing. I love the work that you do. I'm not saying this at face value but because there's a lot of meaning behind it. From your experience, what do you think is stopping people from seeking help? Since we're on this topic.

[silence]

Desmond

Multilayered question. Needs a multilayered answer!

MK

Exactly. We know stigmas are always there.

Desmond

It's always there. Going into a deeper level, perhaps it is about compassion. Not necessarily compassion towards others, but compassion towards ourselves. Societal pressures and what being a Singaporean means to each and every one of us . . . I don't know if this is something that both of you or a lot of people feel, but at least in the circle I'm in, there is this inherent pressure to succeed.

MK

Yeah, the Singaporean dream.

Desmond

Yeah, there's this pressure to push yourself. There are very clear markers of success. This overbearing pressure to perform. In an environment like that, it will breed this perspective of *I cannot be weak, it's a dog-eat-dog world.* We grow up in a very competitive environment.

MK

Correct. Results kind of dictate your worth, your value in society. People actually take it upon themselves to use results to determine the value of their psyche, their whole life.

Desmond

It does! And I'm not saying that we should change the system or anything like that, definitely not. But there are reasons why Singaporeans find ourselves in this position. Like what you're saying, if we tag these measures of success to how we value ourselves, then inherently that's going to be a problem.

MK

Because we're always comparing ourselves with the world and there are always going to be people better than you.

Desmond

Then comes this fear and aversion to admitting defeat. Admitting that at the end of the day we are still human. Admitting that at the end of the day we all make mistakes. Admitting that at the end of the day we're all broken in some ways. There's no one in this world who's not broken.

MK

Takes a lot of courage to acknowledge that.

Desmond

Yeah. It appears in psychological literature as well. Irvin Yalom is one of the famous ones. He's a psychotherapist and in one of his books, he calls us what he coins as 'broken healers', and it's important to take the stance that we all come from a broken place. There's no one in this world who hasn't suffered. But what that also means is that there's nothing wrong with saying that, 'Hey, I'm in a difficult place, it's hard for me to do this on my own, and I just want someone around because I don't want to be alone in this'.

What I often hear from people who come to see a psychologist for the first time in their entire life is that there's so much on their shoulders. The pressure is so much that even when I'm here with them, some of them can't even say that 'I can't do this anymore'. They feel like they still have to wear a mask and put up a front to say that 'I can still keep going'.

MK

Ironically it doesn't matter what titles you carry. You could be a CEO of a company, you could be a manager working nine to five. You could be a student. You could be a housewife.

Desmond

The demographic that I see, because of the charges in private practice, is typically people from the middle to higher-income bracket. But the clinic also does things like lowered fees and pro-bono work. But what I'm trying to say is that it doesn't matter who you are, where you come from, how much resources you have. Mental health difficulties are struggles that everyone goes through. It's just that when you come from a less fortunate background, there is a lot more inherent stress, definitely. And this is the unfortunate truth. The reality is that mental health difficulties do impact the lower income a lot more.

MK

Because for people in the lower-income group, they're fighting for survival.

Si Qi

The hierarchy of needs, right?

Desmond

Yeah. But of course, not dismissing any of the difficulties that the higher brackets experience.

MK

Correct, because they have their own set of issues too. All this can be traced by statistics and works that psychotherapists have done.

Out of curiosity, what's the distinction between a psychologist and a psychiatrist?

Desmond

Aha! That's a very common question.

MK

That's a question I have in my space!

Desmond

It's exactly when questions like this are asked that makes the level of education out there so apparent.

So a psychiatrist is a medical doctor that specializes in psychiatry. So they do their training as a medical degree first and then they specialize and become a psychiatrist. They have to go to medical school. But this also means that the way in which they approach mental health is very different.

Psychiatrists come from a very biological perspective. Which is interesting and probably another conversation for another day because the first psychotherapist was a psychiatrist. Freud, Irvin Yalom, they were all psychiatrists. It's just that the field developed and moved to a more medical model and took on a biological perspective. This is why psychiatrists and psychologists work hand in hand. It's not to say one is better than the other, it's just that we target different things.

MK

I still don't understand the distinction!

Desmond

Okay, so. One of the famous models that we use to approach any kind of mental health difficulty is what we call a biopsychosocial model. This means that any form of mental illness or mental health difficulty is not just one alone.

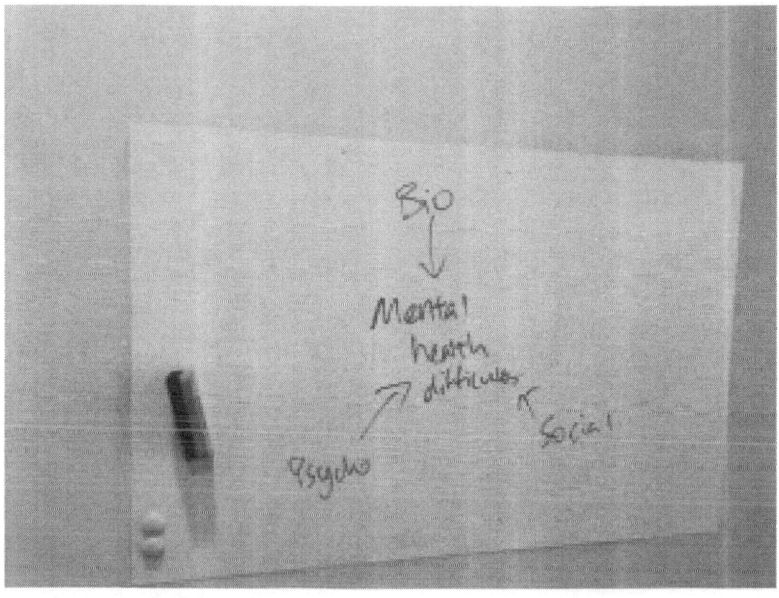

MK

Got it, I recognize that!

Desmond

And this is demonstrated by the evidence to show that medication alone won't solve everything. Therapy alone, sometimes, doesn't solve everything either. The best evidence we have out there is that we need a combination of these three things. Why? Because everything matters. So psychiatrists mainly treat the biology of it. This is where you hear things about brain chemicals and psychiatric drugs. However, just because I take a pill, doesn't mean my problems go away—

MK

Exactly!

Desmond

It doesn't mean my environment changes. It doesn't mean the way in which I relate to my environment changes either. This is where us psychologists come in. We deal with the psychological parts and the social parts sometimes. At least in private settings like this, it's a lot more focused on the psychological parts. But if you go to a public healthcare setting, most of the time mental health treatments happen in multidisciplinary teams. Sometimes the social part is dealt with by a social worker. We all work as a team together to help make shifts and changes.

I get this question a lot too, from my patients. An analogy I like to use is this: imagine any kind of mental health difficulty as if you're drowning in water. Medications help you keep your head above water so you can breathe. Therapy teaches you how to swim. So you can't have one without the other. I can't teach you how to swim if you're drowning. What the medications are meant to do is alleviate the symptoms.

Si Qi

I wanted to ask you. Interestingly enough, you have not mentioned any specific mental health conditions like depression or anxiety, and I think that's one misconception people have, that one needs to be depressed or have anxiety before they are considered to have poor mental health.

Sometimes we may experience symptoms, but they're not serious enough to be considered a mental illness, and because of that, people ignore it or don't do anything about it. How do we change that?

Desmond

First things first. We all feel depressed, we all feel anxious, at some level. All of us do. But what differentiates a mental illness from it not being a mental illness is the level of dysfunction it causes. A mental illness really becomes a mental illness when functional impairment happens. That means that you're no longer able to go to work, you're no longer able to do the things you used to do, you're no longer able to meet friends, your family. Whatever you used to be able to do before, you're no longer able to do because of what you're feeling or experiencing, then that is a cause for concern.

But you're right. Usually by that point, it's quite dysfunctional. Because you're busy putting out fire at that stage. So prevention is always better than dealing with the aftermath. This is where earlier we touched on self-care and things like that, it's important to not just do do do and achieve achieve achieve, and not take a step back and look at how you're treating and taking care of yourself. Essentially this is what therapy as a long-term goal is supposed to achieve. There are different kinds of therapies but the common theme of what each therapy seeks to achieve is that it seeks to build awareness of our internal world.

Because often the principles we use to interact in our external world don't apply when it comes to internal work. For example, what do you do when you get a headache? You take Panadol. You do everything you can to get rid of that headache. But when I take that principle, where I do everything I can to get rid of pain, and apply it to emotional pain, it doesn't work the same. I can try to distract myself, watch Netflix, go out with my friends, go drinking, or any other unhealthy coping methods. At the end of the day, what I'm really trying to do is numb it out, avoid it, just like how I'm trying to use Panadol to get rid of the headache. It doesn't work that way! We have to take a different approach to emotional pain. It's not about getting rid of it, but about learning how to live with it.

MK

I think we have to understand what we're feeling in the first place because we live our whole lives being trained how to use our head in school, but no one ever taught us how to feel.

Our understanding of emotions is so limited. We think we're feeling angry, we think we're feeling happy, we think we're feeling sad. But we don't recognize that these emotions have layers. We can't identify and pinpoint exactly what we're feeling. And who says they're mutually exclusive? We can experience all of these emotions at the same time! And that's why people are conflicted. They don't have the means to understand that. They don't have the awareness. They don't know how to cope with it when they're experiencing it all at one shot.

Desmond

These things are usually taught by parents. This is why parenting is so important. There's so much literature out there that shows that parenting can dictate a child's development, and even predict the child's outcomes in life. That's how important this is. What you've just described is called building emotional vocabulary, being able to identify what you're feeling.

A lot of our behaviour is influenced by the way we feel. Because we feel a certain way, we do certain things. That's why it's so important to correctly identify what we're feeling. Ideally, the parent is supposed to help the child identify their emotions. For example, my son is throwing a huge tantrum because I didn't buy him a toy that he wants and he's saying things like 'I hate you daddy! I don't want you anymore! Why don't you buy me the toy!' and so on. What the child is seemingly expressing is anger. As a parent, you're supposed to help the child identify what he's feeling. You can say something like 'Hey, I know you're really disappointed right now, but expressing your disappointment in this way is not okay'. You let the child tell you what they're feeling, and you help hold the space. And when the child calms down, you basically help the child regulate his emotions. But what you just did is help the child identify that actually *what I'm feeling is not just anger. I feel disappointed, because I didn't get what I want. And because I feel disappointed, the anger comes along too.* All this starts from young. But unfortunately, not everyone—

MK

Has that kind of training or conscious parenting. I mean emotional education is not even part of the syllabus. Our parents or even the previous generation might not even know.

Desmond

Yeah! Parenting is a skill. I sometimes encounter perspectives that say parenting is inborn. The paternal and maternal instinct, yes. The feeling of wanting to protect your child, wanting the best for your child is inborn. But raising a child, parenting, is a skill. And it's important that you, as much as you're able to, based on your circumstances, educate yourself about parenting and how it affects your child. All this is part of psychology. I don't work with children specifically, but I have colleagues who focus solely on children and parenting.

Si Qi

I found it really interesting when you mentioned that it's our feelings that affect how we behave and react to the world because usually we think of it as the world affecting us rather than the other way around.

Desmond

Yeah! This is what we call a feedback loop. How you feel informs how you behave, but how you behave and the reaction of the world also influences how you feel. So it's a feedback loop. Sometimes we don't know that we're stuck in this circle.

MK

It's like a loop. It's the same as playing computer games.

Desmond

Yeah yeah yeah!

MK

Or programming! I always tell people that, when I'm running classes, that we're in a loop.

It's like a person who stands here [points in front of the grey cup] looking up will see a grey wall. But from our angle we can see that it is a grey cup. The problem is the people who are down here seeing this as a grey wall can't see this as a cup. There's no way, unless they have the ability to bring themselves up.

Desmond

Perspective matters! A metaphor that I like to use also is that before you came into this room, you have always worn red-tinted glasses. And if I asked you what the colour of this wall is, you'd probably tell me it's red. If I tell you that it's white, you'd probably think that I'm crazy.

MK

So the question is, do we have the openness to re-examine our lives? Do we have the courage or even self-love to recognize that *hey, maybe I'm actually wearing tinted lenses?* And this pair of tinted lenses is what was being constructed our whole lives, especially from zero to nine years old. What we experience later on in life just reinforces the way we look at the world.

We see the world for who we are rather than what the world is. We end up creating endless misunderstandings in our relationships as a result of that. It still boils down to whether we have the courage to take these lenses off, to re-examine our lives, so that we can relearn who we are, and who we are not.

These days, people often associate their jobs, their career, as part of their identity. But COVID happened. A banker who has worked as a banker for the last sixteen years, who suddenly loses his job, is going to feel confused because he has always referred to himself as a banker. Only now he realizes that there's a void, an emptiness. And it's not going to be long before he spirals down if he doesn't have the necessary systems and structures in place.

Desmond

It's interesting. What you just described is one of the things we work on in some therapies. There are many different names, but the basic idea is that when you are too fused to a certain identity, to the point that it informs how you relate to people, how you relate to the world, how you relate to yourself, there is nothing left for you when you lose that identity. At certain levels, it can get quite unhealthy. That's why it's important to recognize that you are able to have different identities.

MK

You're not fixed or born with one personality.

Desmond

Personality as a construct is fluid, anyway.

MK

That's why people are so caught up with personality tests and horoscopes. They need to feel like somebody understands them and that they are wanted.

Desmond

In some sense, it is important to build different parts of yourself. Who are you as a son? Who are you as a daughter? Who are you as a father? Who are you as a mother? Who are you as a friend? Who are you as a lover?

It's important to build these parts and give them adequate attention even though yes, it is challenging when you have to prioritize work over, say, family, due to your circumstances. But doesn't mean that we neglect the other parts of us. Yeah. Which it's why it's complicated—

MK

I wouldn't say complicated, I would say complex.

Desmond

Complex, it is complex. That's why therapy takes time.

MK

It's like if you tell so many things to a person in a short span of time, they don't have the capacity or bandwidth to understand it for what it is.

Desmond

And everyone's experience is different too, which also prevents people from coming in. I tell them that you can't just see me one time and feel better. That's not how it works. It's not the same as seeing a doctor for physical illnesses. Let's say you're thirty. You can't come in here and squeeze thirty years of your life into an hour and say 'I feel better now'. That's not how it works. It's a process. And it being a process means that there will have to be certain levels of commitment. But not everyone's at a place to do that and that's okay. There are many people who come in and leave therapy and they come back again at different phases in their life, which is fine too. But recognizing that it's a process and to properly give it time for it to develop and work through that process is important as well.

Si Qi

I'm wondering if you could—because you shared your personal story about contemplating suicide at twelve—share some words with twelve-year-old students who've faced a setback in life?

Desmond

I don't know if this will apply to everyone. But connecting to my twelve-year-old self, I think what I would have liked at that point in time is for someone to reach out. Not just for anyone, but someone I felt like I would be able to go to. Because at that point in time I felt like I didn't have anyone to go to. I felt quite alone in that, because everyone was telling me how I was worthless, basically.

At the end of the day, you are the expert of your own life. Who am I to say otherwise? You could give me an autobiographical account of your entire life and yet I may not fully understand exactly what you went through and what you felt. It's not my place to tell you how to live your life. Rather, it's about having a safe space for us to explore this together, where in your own life, you may or may not have had that kind of opportunity. Not every one of us is lucky enough to have a family member, friend or partner who is able to hold us in this way. Of course, there are a lot more things to think about! Being here, there's also an advantage of me being a third party.

And so, for the twelve-year-olds out there, this is a message that if you're willing to talk, if you're willing to tell people, there will be people who are willing to listen, even if they may not be your family. There are counsellors in schools. There are teachers in schools. There will be adults who are willing to listen. Know that you are not alone in this. Many people feel the same way you do, and there's nothing wrong with that. The important thing is to continue building and living the life that you want.

CHAPTER 2

Living True To Who You Are

By Camellia Wong, Co-founder, Principal Psychologist, InPsychful

As an EM3[3] student in primary school, Camellia grew up being labelled as a failure by her teachers and principals. She later found herself drawn to forensic psychology because she felt that most people were only attracted to the nice and dandy side of life, and were quick to condemn and alienate those who they perceived as flawed without trying to understand why they behaved the way they did. Currently running her own private practice, she explains how the pressure to meet societal labels and expectations creates stress and a lack of self-acceptance, and how our mental health and wellbeing is affected if we spend our lives living for everyone else but ourselves.

[3] EM3: The stream of students found to have difficulty with English language and mathematics subjects in primary school. This stream was discontinued in 2009.

CARRY YOUR OWN WEIGHT

Si Qi

How did you get started working in the mental health space?

Camellia

So it started when I was about seventeen or eighteen. I took a gap year from my studies after graduating from O levels because I didn't want to just go into a course to study for the sake of studying. It was not easy for my parents to accept that, but I wanted to make sure that whatever course I chose was going to be something that I really wanted to pursue. Of course, I wasn't just lazing around. I was working at the time, and I like to read quite a lot and that was when I stumbled upon forensic psychology.

So at that time, I was deciding between forensic psychology or law, and I decided to go with psychology, and that has been the goal for a really long time—to pursue it postgrad and become a forensic psychologist. I started to realize that a lot of people give attention to victims and people who are suffering, and they view offenders as people who are more aggressive, more violent, and for lack of a better word, the rubbish of society. Nobody wants to work with this population, whether it's challenging kids, challenging teenagers, or adults who broke the law, because people don't see that they are also suffering, albeit in a different way from victims.

Looking back, I think a lot of it has got to do with my personal story. At a young age, I was already seen as a failure in life. I didn't do well academically. The principals and teachers called my parents every day. And when I was in primary school, I was in EM3, so it was a very quick label that people who had such traits would not succeed in life. I think the reason why I was drawn to forensic psychology was because people tend to look at the nice and dandy side of things, and typically people with a lot of flaws are just immediately condemned and nobody really bothers to find a way to work with them. So that was how I started out as a forensic psychologist with MSF[4].

Of course, now that I have my own practice, it's really about working with individuals who want to seek therapy, and not just because they are mentally ill, but also because they've reached out to friends and family regarding certain things that they may be struggling with and they find that they are at their wit's end, so they might think *maybe it's time I turned to a professional.*

Si Qi

Thank you for sharing that. So you were actually the first person who introduced to us the idea that there's a difference between mental illness and mental wellness. Can you share more about that?

Camellia

So mental health is like physical health. We do things to prevent illnesses—we try to eat healthier, we try to get proper sleep, and we try to exercise regularly. Some people will go to the extent of getting a gym trainer, signing up for yoga classes, things like that. That is looking after physical health. A physical illness happens when somebody is diagnosed with an illness, and similarly for mental illness, it is when somebody is clinically diagnosed with a mental illness. But when we are not in a good state emotionally or mentally, it doesn't mean we're mentally ill. People can have symptoms of depression, but they may not meet the clinical diagnosis criteria, because there are times in our life when we feel sad. Let's say, if we go through a breakup or we lose someone dear to us, it's natural for us to feel sad. It's natural for us to grieve. But because the media

---

[4] MSF: Ministry of Social and Family Development

has portrayed this image that the moment somebody's a little bit more quiet, shy, or withdrawn, it's as though there are dark clouds hovering over them.

Sometimes, the individual is shy. People also view introverts as having a lot of problems compared to extroverts. But introverts themselves actually can be quite extroverted when they are in a group that they feel comfortable with.

Si Qi

Everybody goes through difficult emotions, but why is it so difficult for people to acknowledge that or ask for help? What is the stigma in that?

Camellia

It's a lot to do with our culture. A lot of times, we are taught from young to not share about the difficulties we are going through. If the family is going through a difficult time, we are taught to not talk about it. We are taught to carry the weight on our own. We are taught that if we talk about our problems, it means that we are weak, that we don't know how to solve our issues. But the truth is, humans are not designed to be on our own. Humans are very social creatures and sometimes, we may not even be looking for solutions, we may just be looking for someone to talk to so that we can let it out. Sometimes, when we talk about certain things, we may get the chance to internally process what is happening unconsciously rather than *oh, if I tell you, you give me a solution.*

Si Qi

I don't know about other people, but when I was at some of the lower points in my life, it never crossed my mind that I could talk to someone else other than my friends. And I'm wondering why is that? For some reason you would just keep going on, doing the same thing over and over again, living your life as it is.

Camellia

It's a lot of things. I've also had clients ask me, 'Therapy is such a Western concept, how does that impact our values as Asians?' We need to understand that these ways of treatment, or rather, how we do therapy, has that cultural consideration as well. We don't just take something from the West and apply the approach wholesale. We take cultural upbringing into consideration. But it's harder for us because of the whole outlook that if you ask for help, it means you're weak, that problems are not good because you have to look like a perfect individual that has got everything together. A lot of clients also ask me, 'Cam, since you're a psychologist, I'm sure you don't have a lot of problems, right?' Because as a psychologist, you're expected to be able to manage your own problems.

Si Qi

Yeah, because you have the toolbox.

Camellia

Yeah. So I said, 'Well, I do have problems. It's not that I don't, because I'm also human like any one of you.' But it's just about knowing how to put into practice what I've learned. And it's not always easy. Some situations are harder, some situations are easier, but therapists use the same coping strategies that we would recommend too.

WHEN WHO YOU WANT TO BE IS NOT WHO YOU'RE EXPECTED TO BE

Si Qi

And I think in Singapore, we have our own version of problems where we strive really hard to hit certain milestones in life, like

BTO[5], ROM[6], to the point that if you don't go down that path then *who are you?* Are you even a good daughter, good son, good parent, good partner, or whatever, right? We have all these labels and we run ourselves to the ground trying to fit that mould.

Camellia

Yeah. Especially since our culture is one that, no matter how old we grow, it's common that we live with our parents—married, not married, young, or old. Sometimes, the struggle comes when people want a sense of autonomy by living on their own or making their own decisions, and that's difficult. I mean, the truth is, living in Singapore is not cheap. Owning your own flat is also not cheap. And let's say, if a person is single and wants to apply for a flat, they have to wait quite a while, until they're thirty-five. So for the generations to come, the sense of autonomy is something that a lot of them want and our culture doesn't exactly quite support that.

Si Qi

Why is autonomy so important?

Camellia

Because it builds a sense of identity. If we always remain in the identity that is attached to parents, or how our parents view us as a child, then it hinders competency level or how far we can go in terms of our competency in many aspects of our life.

Si Qi

I recall, in our first ever conversation with you, you shared with us that there is this perception that the previous generation always

[5] BTO: Build to Order (public housing in Singapore)

[6] ROM: Registry of Marriages

feels that the younger generation is weaker. That everyone is just getting weaker and weaker over time

Camellia

Yes, there's that labelling going on. There are also a lot of labels on the younger generation like *oh, you have everything, during my time, my Internet was still dial-up, it was so slow. Google didn't exist, now you have everything.* The comparison is always *my time, we didn't have this, and now you have all this.*

The younger generation, in my opinion, actually have it harder because there are so many things that are expected of them. The younger generation is expected to perform much better, they're expected to move at a faster pace, and they're expected to be grateful. But some things you gain, some things you also lose.

Si Qi

What do you think we have lost?

Camellia

I think a lot of us have lost the ability to let loose a little bit—for kids to go out and play, for adults to say 'It's okay if I want to take some time off work, spend some me time away from the kids, away from my parents.' There's a lot of responsibility that this generation has to shoulder.

Si Qi

There's a disconnect with the self?

Camellia

I think there's a lot of disconnect with the self. There are a lot more responsibilities that we need to fulfil. Like what you said, we have to go through the proper academic route. The responsibility and hope is that we go through university. After we go through university, the expectation is to find a job. When you find a job, the expectation is to start providing for the family. After that, if the person doesn't have a partner, find a partner. Then the next step is to get married. After you get married, the next thing people ask you is *when are you going to have kids?* After you have kids, there'll be a whole long list of expectations like *why didn't you send your kids for tuition? Why didn't you send your kid for that enrichment class? Why is your kid like this, why is your kid like that?* So when do we actually live our lives?

Si Qi

I think this is a struggle and internal conflict that a lot of people have, that the person that you want to be is different from the person your parents expected you to become. But we were brought up by them. How did we end up being in conflict with ourselves?

Camellia

I think that there are multiple factors why. Starting from the unit closest to us—our family, sometimes our family may not be supportive of what we want to do or who we want to become. I'm fortunate that my mum allowed us to explore whatever we were interested in. While the school and teachers were calling her every other day, she was like *it's okay, she's a child, let her go and play, let her go and explore.* And she was not comfortable—she was not happy that I took one year off after O levels to find out what I wanted to do, but she allowed it. So that exploration first starts from the family. If they allow that.

Then of course, it is also about having to build that resilience in the child when they face multiple challenges in their life. And why resilience is such a vast word is because, for one, we're not good at talking about failure. We're always chasing after society's idea of what it wants us to be so that we won't be a failure. If you finish university, you get a job, you find a partner, you get married, you have kids, you send your kids to all the co-curricular stuff at a young age, then your kid does well—that is success in our terms.

Si Qi

And if you're single at forty, you're a failure in life.

Camellia

Yeah. You get questioned. And people end up not wanting to socialize with family because they get questioned. So how do you talk about failure? What even is failure? Where do we peg this to? If I'm forty and single but I'm happy, I'm doing what I want, I'm achieving my goals, I can provide for the family, I'm happy playing whatever role it is I'm playing, then is that considered failure? And failure to whom?

Si Qi

That's a really good question: failure to whom? We spend all our lives trying to live the life, or become the version of ourselves that our parents want of—

Camellia

Or what society wants. I once met somebody who told me that my child's academic achievement is a reflection of how successful I am as a parent. And I'm like, wow, that's such a harsh thing to say to yourself, because there are a lot of things that your child can achieve other than academic results. It stuck with me because I wonder how that child is doing. I imagine it must be quite hard, right? If their life is purely based on academic achievements. Well, it's going to be tough on both parties. To a lot of kids, they just want to have some time to be a kid.

DARE TO TRY THINGS OUT

Si Qi

And I think the thing we have a hard time dealing with, other than failure, is uncertainty.

Camellia

Oh yes!
[Camellia laughs]

Si Qi

Because going through this academic route gives us, well, you could say a false sense of security, but there is a good measure of stability and predictability to be had in following the academic pathway. I remember when I was in school, I totally couldn't imagine exploring an alternative path!

Camellia

Yeah so a lot of times, we're lacking in that real-world skill set or decision-making process. A lot of the interns and some of the ex-students that I used to work with would reach out to me because they don't know what to do after they've graduated. A lot of them just know that *okay, I want to be a psychologist, I need to do postgrad, full stop*. And I tell them to go and try different kinds of internships, get a research-related internship, or get an internship that lets you interact with the population that you want to work with. If you don't know what population you want to work with, volunteer for different populations. Try things out. Find out which one you're more drawn to.

A lot of them also have the concern of time. *How much time do I really have or can afford to explore before choosing a path?* Then the other concern is *what if this is not the path that I want?*

Si Qi

Well, then you're screwed because you just spent your entire life studying for it and you even got a degree for it!

[laughter]

Camellia

Yeah so, it's being able to accept the process of trying things out.

My mum once asked me what I would do if I couldn't get into postgrad. I said 'No, I'll make sure that I try until I get in'. She shared with me that she was very worried after I graduated, because it was the first time in my life that I told her I didn't have a backup plan. She was quite amazed when I made it and she asked me why I was so certain. I told her that it was my goal all along and I made sure I achieved it. And she said, 'What if it's different from what you've been doing all this while?' Because prior to being a psychologist, I was doing a lot of adventure education, character development programmes and training. I told her that even if I were to return to training, I'll be equipped with more skill sets, so I'm not losing anything. But if I don't go and try, it'll always be a question of *what if?*

It's also what we can live with. For me, I'd rather go and try than to live the rest of my life asking myself *what if I had done postgrad, would my life be different?*

Si Qi

I think it's really a balancing act. On one hand you have to manage the uncertainty, and on the other hand, you've got to be very determined to achieve your goals. It's also about trusting yourself that you'll see this to the end.

Camellia

Looking back when I was going to go into forensic psychology, everyone told me not to. Even my closest friends told me that no one in the world is going to hire you. So I'm also a certified badminton coach and I've been coaching for a while. My friends were like why don't you go into sports psychology? Why would you want to do forensic psychology when you're a coach? Why are you deviating into something that is totally different from what you have been doing for the past thirteen years? But this has been my dream and it was the course that I really wanted.

Si Qi

I have a question that might be a little difficult to answer.

Camellia

Sure.

Si Qi

Do you need to be in a more privileged position to be able to try things out and figure out what you want to do in life?

Camellia

I don't really know. Because there are less privileged individuals who can achieve their goals, just maybe in a longer time frame than those who are privileged. I think it's how we view ourselves and how much we want to pursue it. Because there are people from privileged families who end up not having the same level of achievement as those who came from less privileged families.

Si Qi

Yeah. I asked that because some people reading this will think *I don't have the time to try internships for one year, I need to get a job now.* I think there's a lot of pressure in society lah.

Camellia

It's a very good question that I ask my interns who are graduating and looking for jobs. *How urgent does your family need the money? How urgent do you need the money?* If your answer is *no, I need to get a job immediately*, then I say *okay then you need to be strategic about how you find your first job so that you can move up the career ladder to get you where you want to go.* It requires strategic planning. It also requires strategic research. If you have the luxury of trying multiple internships, go ahead. It's good to start trying and researching earlier.

Si Qi

I remember when I was eighteen, I had no idea what the hell I wanted to do. And even after I finished university, I still had no idea what I wanted to do. And when I went to work and I asked my colleagues what they wanted to do, they didn't know too. And we are working already, you know!
[laughter]

Si Qi

So how can we connect with ourselves to figure out what we want to do in life?

Camellia

Try lor.
[Si Qi laughs]

Camellia

Because like I said, since the earlier parts of my life, from primary all the way through secondary school, I was already deemed a failure in life. So what's so bad about failing another time?
[laughter]

Camellia

It doesn't even mean anything to me, because it was already such a huge part of my life. And when you fail, when you're at the bottom, the only way to go is up. Of course, you can choose to stay down there too, because sometimes it's easier to stay there than to stand up and try again.

Si Qi

So it was a blessing in disguise!

Camellia

Yeah, it was definitely a blessing. I mean, academically, my future was very bleak. Diploma was good enough for me. I didn't even think about getting a degree.

So if you try and it doesn't work out, then fine, we go back to the drawing board. How else can we improve this situation? What did we learn from the past? Rather than just saying *okay we failed, full stop, try harder next time*. But try harder at what? Do better at what? You mean we didn't try hard enough? Sometimes we've already tried our best, but we just didn't make it.

Si Qi

It can be difficult to have that clarity because we can get so consumed by the pain of failure that we can't see anything else. To fail and say *okay, let's evaluate, let's move forward in a better way*—I think we need to learn how to do that.

Camellia

And for me, I always attribute it to the values my mum imparted to me. She always told me that she can work hard, earn as much money as she can to pay for other co-curricular programmes since I wasn't doing well academically, but at the end of the day, it's still my choice whether I want to do anything. So I got to decide if I wanted tuition or not. I was getting average grades from secondary one to four, but it was not until secondary five that I decided I wanted tuition. When I made the decision for myself, I also valued the time with the tutor more.

This was something that my mum taught me. Parents can provide, but at the end of the day, what we want to do with our lives is our decision to make. I think my mum's parenting style took a lot of courage out of her, to let us explore and teach us to be accountable for our choices.

THE IDEAL SELF AND THE TRUE SELF

Si Qi

So this conversation about being yourself and finding out what you want to do . . . How is this linked to mental health?

Camellia

It's very much linked to mental health. There's this thing that we call the 'ideal self' and the 'true self'. If we have an ideal image of who we want to be, but we know that who we really are is very far from the ideal self, that causes dissonance in us. And people tend to struggle with that dissonance.

For example, I have a friend who believes she is extroverted, but she's actually very introverted. She just wants to believe that she is extroverted because she believes that people who are extroverted are perceived better in society. So she tries very hard to be extroverted, but more often than not she just gets exhausted and irritated. So that's a constant struggle for her. *Who am I? Why do I want to take on society's perception that extroverts are better than introverts? Why do I think that introverts are socially inept?* Which is also not necessarily true.

Si Qi

And it's not easy to answer those questions. After a while, a lot of us give up or feel very resigned trying to find our life's purpose or trying to find ourselves because it's so hard! Perhaps it even gets to the point where we're so disconnected with ourselves that we don't even know what we're looking for anymore.

Camellia

The thing I always ask my clients is 'When was the last time you sat with yourself?' And a lot of them look at me like *what kind of question is that?* For many Singaporeans, even when we go on a holiday, we bring our work laptops with us, we're checking our emails, we're still responding in work group chats because we feel guilty if we don't. There's no time to disconnect, there's no time to be with the self, there's no time to be with loved ones. Life just becomes clockwork. But when we pause and think, we sometimes don't even understand the purpose of that clockwork. So that's one of the questions that I always ask my clients. 'When was the last time you sat with yourself?' And you'll be amazed, some of them tell me 'I don't dare. I don't dare to see. What if I'm not the person that I think I am?'

Si Qi

It's like a Pandora's box. But all of us have one, right?

Camellia

All of us have it. All of us have flaws. All of us have sides of us that we like, sides of us that we don't like. It's a question of *when do we come into acceptance of who we are? When do we decide that we want to be better versions of ourselves, and in which aspects?*

Si Qi

Yeah. I just find it incredible that even for me personally, before I plucked up the courage to start finding my purpose, I couldn't really see the link between finding my purpose and my mental wellness. But there was a huge shift the moment I started to even just chip away at this idea I had. I was excited about waking up, excited about life, and that translated to a lot of positive effects on the state of my daily mental and emotional wellness.

But you're right, sometimes we just get so caught up with the cycle of work that we don't have the space to figure things out.

Camellia

It's also very different between generations. If you look at the baby boomer generation, they had to work very hard because the focus was to put food on the table. Their motivation was to allow the next generation to have a better life. Now that people in my generation have a better life, we want to provide the same for the next generation. But then a lot of us are also starting to wonder whether this clockwork of wake up, get dressed, go to work, sleep, repeat, is something that we really want. What's the meaning behind that? Is that all to life?

My interns and ex-students will ask me, 'What if it doesn't turn out to be what I want? Then I just wasted X number of years in the initial years of my career pursuing something that I don't even want'.

So then what's lacking here is the cognitive flexibility to say that 'Yes, I worked in industry A and I realized that it was not what I wanted, what are my skill sets that will help me shift towards industry B?' There are definitely skill sets that you've learnt that can be transferred to your new workplace. We don't always start on a blank slate all over again.

Si Qi

I want to go back to the idea of the ideal and true self a bit more. How does the ideal self come about?

Camellia

So there are a lot of factors. There are environmental factors, there are also social factors. Your family tells you who you have to be. Society tells you that you need to be this person or that person. Your social group may tell you to be a certain person too. Sometimes people put all that up for a show because if they don't, they may think or believe that they're not going to be accepted. But deep down, they know that they're not that kind of person.

Si Qi

So should we be pursuing the ideal self?

Camellia

It's more about bringing the true self and ideal self together, where it can meet and be one identity rather than saying I choose one or the other.

For example, let's say somebody's true self is an introvert, but their ideal self is to be an extrovert. They know they can't get there because that's not really who they are, and they feel very drained and they don't enjoy putting up a front. Then the question is *how can they still have that external portrayal but still be who they are?* So maybe it's about being a functional introvert, where you can still carry yourself well in public settings.

Si Qi

Right. So what about the true self, where does it come from?

Camellia

It comes from you. Who you are and what you can accept.

Si Qi

Is it something you're born with?

Camellia

No, we all develop parts of ourselves as we grow. As we grow, we interact with the environment, we interact with people. It's not entirely nurture, and it's not entirely nature. It actually comes together because it's not as direct.

Si Qi

I'm just trying to understand this so we can all get this concept. So the true self also includes things that you learn and pick up?

Camellia

Yeah, your experiences that you pick up over time.

Si Qi

Right. So how come we are comfortable with the true self, but we can't embody the ideal self traits that we desire?

Camellia

Sometimes they don't even like their true self.

Si Qi

Ahh . . .

Camellia

Sometimes people don't even like their true self. If a person is naturally more shy or quieter, then maybe they'll always wish that they're like that classmate who is more outspoken. Or maybe this person always wants to be with the popular crowd, even though deep down they know that they're not like that crowd of people. There are parts of our true self that we know we don't reconcile with, even things that we don't know.

Si Qi

It's quite complex.

Camellia

Yeah, there are a lot of cogs in the wheel.

Si Qi

So what happens when you bring the ideal and the true self together?

Camellia

One, the individual will have a lot more clarity about who they are. It also sets a greater foundation of who they are, why they make certain decisions, why they behave a certain way, and things they want to pursue. Of course, this is just one part of a much larger picture. Sometimes it also gives them a lot more clarity on how they want to address certain issues they might be having.

Si Qi

Right. Wow, it's so complex because there's so many factors that come into play. Society, every single person you meet, shaping you and your inner world.

Camellia

Humans are complex.

BE COMFORTABLE WITH THE DISCOMFORT

Si Qi

Yeah. I truly think it's a worthwhile endeavour to look into yourself and find out who you are. Mental health is for everyone. So how can we start to address the stigmas preventing people from doing that?

Camellia

I think the very first thing is just being comfortable asking for help, to know that asking for help is okay. A lot of times, people don't want to share with their friends and family because they don't want to burden others. This word 'burden' comes up a lot. *I don't want to burden other people. I don't want to trouble other people. They have their own problems. What makes me so special that they'll help me through mine?*

We need to reframe those thoughts. If somebody who's important in your life comes to you with a problem they're going through, will you tell them that *hey you're such a burden you know, I got my own problems too.* The truth is many of us won't. Another thing we need to do before we share with others is to learn how to talk about our problems. It's not that we don't want to reach out, but sometimes we don't even know where to start or how to start talking about our problems. Everything is in our head! We don't know where to start.

Si Qi

Because we've suppressed them?

Camellia

Not just suppressed. Some of us may not even have that model image of *how do I talk about my problems?*

Think about the first person that came to you to talk about their problems, how was it like for you?
[silence]

Si Qi

Well, this really takes me back. I've not thought about this before. I think the earliest memory I can recall was probably in primary school. I had a friend who had a pretty good family background. Her parents were in good professions, or what I perceived to be good when I was a kid. I remember being a little surprised when she told me about her family problems. I didn't expect her to have that.

Camellia

Yeah. So sometimes when we look at our own circle, we don't expect it, right? Because some things look so normal, or what we perceive to be normal. And nobody really teaches us how to talk about our problems. It's always *come to me when you have a problem.* Sure, I go to you, and then? Would you facilitate the conversation? Would you ask me about my problems? It's always the one who needs to talk to somebody who needs to initiate the conversation. Why not ask the people around us *how are you doing?* Sometimes that's all it takes for someone to open up. We've not been taught how to support others.

Si Qi

We're not comfortable with difficult emotions.

Camellia

Yeah. Or sometimes people want to help, but they don't know that helping or showing support can mean just sitting there with the other person. Maybe all that the other person wants is just somebody to listen to them. But because we have not been taught how to help, we don't really know how to help. We are quite an outcome-focused society, it's always *okay, what solution can I provide to this individual?* But sometimes they don't need solutions.

Si Qi

And the thing is knowing how to listen and how to be present is not something that is applied to mental-health-related situations only. We can apply these skill sets for many other work, social or personal situations. I think it's really interesting because we've looked at mental health from a very broad perspective.

Camellia

Yeah. It's not as straightforward as *depression means I'm constantly sad. If I have anxiety, means I'm always on edge.* It's not always like that. We're not all flat in our emotions. And in fact, if somebody's flat in their emotions, I will always ask them more questions.

Emotions help us figure out what actually is going on inside us. What is it about this situation that makes us have these feelings?

Si Qi

Yeah, emotional vocabulary is something we don't really have as well.

Camellia

Yeah, we don't. Because that's how we have been taught since young. Sad, happy, angry are the most common ones. A lot of people don't know about the ones in between.

Si Qi

Yeah, so you don't know how to express yourself even if you wanted to.

Camellia

So the expression can sometimes be a bit challenging. But the good thing is that we have improved a lot in terms of stigma. It's not all a lost cause. So, as we go on this journey to address the issue of stigma, it's also about acknowledging the improvements that have been made.

ABOVE ALL, BE TRUE TO YOURSELF

Si Qi

That is true.

Final question. What is one message you would like to leave the readers with about mental health?

Camellia

That everybody goes through difficult times in our lives. That anybody you look at on the streets would have gone through something challenging at some point in their lives. It's part and parcel of life. And in those moments when we are low, it's okay to seek help. It's like reading, right? If somebody's bad at reading or they can't pronounce words, they can find out how to do it.But when it comes to mental health, a lot of things are hidden. Because depression doesn't exactly have a stereotypical face. Anxiety doesn't have a stereotypical face. Anger doesn't have a stereotypical face. It's how the media portrays those faces that gives people the perception of what these mental illnesses are. But everyone goes through their own struggles. Let's say we have a huge quarrel at home. People don't go to work with a sticker on their forehead that says *I just quarrelled with my partner today*. It's more of *okay I'm going to work, I have to be professional, I have to smile*. But inside you're still really upset.

Si Qi

A lot of masks.

Camellia

We all wear a lot of masks. I guess the last thing that I'll say is to be true to yourself before anyone else. To be honest with yourself before anyone else.

CHAPTER 3

If You Don't See It, It Doesn't Mean It's Not There

By Peggy Lim, Social Worker,
TOUCH Community Services

Peggy talks about the mental health challenges faced by youths today, especially in our increasingly complicated digital environment. Mental health conditions are not always obvious and visible—that is why it is important for parents and youths to recognize that mental health exists on a continuum, and there is no shame in having a bad day and needing help with overcoming, dealing, and coping with negative emotions.

STUMBLING INTO MENTAL HEALTH WORK

Si Qi

Could you tell me about your backstory and why you decided to go into mental health work?

Peggy

What made me decide to go into mental-health-related work? That's an interesting question because when I was looking for a job at TOUCH, I wasn't looking for a mental-health-related job in particular. I was simply looking for a position which would allow me to work with youths or youths at risk. At TOUCH, while working with youths, we realized that many of them were struggling to cope with various stressors in their lives which contributed to their mental health being affected. To address this issue, we embarked on developing a mental health education programme for secondary schools. The programme included a group work segment which was designed for us to follow up with youths who have gone for the programme and needed further intervention. That was how I got into mental health work.

As for why I chose youth work—I feel that in every youth, there is a child that they sometimes mask by trying to be an adult. A lot of them do struggle with a lot of emotional pain. The adolescent stage is an especially turbulent time for them, and even more so if they have family issues or mental health issues. They're at a stage where they are constantly trying to figure themselves out and sometimes, they feel very lonely and they feel like they don't have friends or that nobody understands them. There is an inner child hidden in every youth, and it's important to connect with that child who is in need of acceptance and support.

GENERATIONAL DIFFERENCES IN MENTAL HEALTH LITERACY

Si Qi

In your work with youths, what would you say are some of the mental health stigmas that you see happening a lot in this age group?

Peggy

A lot of times I think the stigma comes from families. The reason why I say that is because based on some of the things I've observed, I see that there's a very big cultural difference in terms of mental health literacy now and from maybe thirty years ago. And this difference in societal and cultural expectations creates a lot of disparities between parents' expectations of mental health and children's wellbeing and what the youths think about mental health. This is very important because I do see quite a number of youths asking for help, but they always tell me 'Please don't tell my family, my family wouldn't understand'. I think that thirty years ago, conversations on mental health were almost non-existent. There was no such thing as mental health awareness or education initiatives, but that didn't mean that mental health issues didn't exist. It just wasn't talked about. Mental health issues in the past were probably defined as either you have schizophrenia, or you are crazy, or you're totally not functioning, but actually there are a lot of people with mental health issues who can function, even on a high level.

So this also brings me to the second stigma that I see, which is that if you are functioning well, it means you have no need for mental health treatment, which is not true! I think the concept of a high-functioning person with mental health issues may sound counter intuitive, especially to the older generations. They're like, 'You're okay! You just need to not think so much!' These are some of the things that I hear. Sometimes this may lead to parents not believing their kids and I think they're not coming from a place where they have bad intentions, but it just doesn't make sense to them.

Because of these disparities, it's very hard for families to resonate with the youths completely. But I can see they're trying to because they'll bring their kids for counselling sessions and they'll tell me, 'Actually I don't really know how to deal with it!' I think it is good that they recognize it as a problem for the child. I mean we're not looking for the perfect opinion about mental health, but I think it's about helping people to recognize that this is an integral part of health. Mental health is just as important as physical health. If you're not doing well in terms of your physical health, it will affect your mental health, and vice versa.

Si Qi

I guess that's the thing you know—mental health is, as compared to physical health, very invisible and therefore, you can't really tell. Could you explain how somebody can be functioning well, presenting that they're functioning well on the outside, but still have a mental health condition? How does this coexist?

Peggy

It differs from person to person. Let's talk about the severity of the mental health issue. If the condition is severe, it would affect your performance, your outlook on life, your ability to cope, your ability to motivate yourself when you need to get things done. Secondly, a lot of people, especially in Singapore, or in a society that's very competitive, develop this persona that helps us to cope with the stress. So a lot of people go to work and may put on that persona. Maybe they're on survival mode. Maybe they're actually not feeling well, but they're just trying to make sure they can keep their jobs, that they can finish school. But after they get home at night, when work or school is taken away, they start getting in touch with what's going on within them, and that's when they start experiencing different mental health symptoms.

Unfortunately, a lot of times people feel that at the workplace or in schools, that's not something they can show. And unlike physical health where it's okay for you to rest at home, if you have a mental health issue and people can't see it, they're like, 'Oh you mean you're not going to do anything, you're just going to stay at home?' But there are people who need that time to recover. I mean, if an issue with your physical health requires you to rest and stay in bed, then somebody whose mental health is severely affected would need that rest as well.

MENTAL HEALTH EXISTS ON A CONTINUUM

Si Qi

Yeah, I can relate to that. For me, before I started to learn more about mental health, my understanding of mental health was very narrow. I just thought that having a mental health condition meant being in a depressed state. And what a depressed state would look like if somebody was just crying all the time, or not able to do anything, just sitting around. I didn't realize that there was a spectrum and there are different ways people cope with it and experience mental health.

Peggy

I think mental health is definitely something that exists on a continuum. When I see it that way, it helps me to know that when someone is not feeling too good, it doesn't always mean he or she is having a relapse, or that they have a mental illness.

It's about knowing that we move along this continuum based on the circumstances that we experience, based on the stresses that we experience, based on our ability to cope. When we emerge through a difficult situation and gain new ways to cope, we do move up that continuum in a good way. Being able to see that helps me to know that it's human and it's normal. Sometimes we may have a bad mental health day, but it's not something to be ashamed about, because we all have emotions.

What practicing good mental health habits means to me is being able to take care of yourself. Being able to say no when you need to. And being able to practice self-compassion.

IN A COMPETITIVE SOCIETY, IT SEEMS COUNTERINTUITIVE TO BE KIND TO YOURSELF

Si Qi

So, you talked about how practicing self-compassion is important for our mental health. Could you share a bit more about that?

Peggy

Self-compassion is the ability to be kind to yourself when you notice your shortcomings, when you notice that things didn't go well or didn't go your way. And why it's important is because just being kind to ourselves is not something that's easy to do, especially in an Asian culture. And given how competitive society can be, it almost seems counterintuitive to be kind to yourself when you make a mistake. We grow up knowing that we should always be very hard on ourselves or we'll be punished for our mistakes. Of course, there are certain things that we do where there would be consequences, like *hey, I forgot to do this*, or *I missed out on this at work*.

The reason why being kind to yourself and not judging yourself for making a mistake is important is because if we shame ourselves into growth by criticizing ourselves, by punishing ourselves, by putting ourselves down, it makes the process of growth and change very painful. As human beings, it's natural that we don't want to experience emotional pain. Self-compassion facilitates the opportunity for growth by creating a safe environment for it, which is why it's so important. I would say that self-compassion is something that people should focus more on as compared to self-esteem. Your self-esteem will come naturally when you treat yourself right, when you treat yourself in a kind way. How do we find self-esteem if we shame ourselves into growth? And self-compassion is something that follows you not just when you're doing very well in life, but when you're not doing so well too. Shame has a lot of negative effects and it could contribute to mental health issues when somebody is exposed to very prolonged and intense shaming. And it's not because the person is not strong enough to handle the shame.

SCHOOL, FRIENDS, AND THE INTERNET

Si Qi

I want to go back to youths. What are some of the reasons why youths experience mental health conditions today?

Peggy

A very common one is academic stress. Some of the youths that I know tend to have unrealistic and unattainable expectations. Many times, they may feel like *it's either I get this grade or I'm nothing. If I don't get into this school, there's no hope for me in the future*. A lot of them feel that they don't deserve to take a break because that would affect their grades. Their self-perceptions and their identity are based on their grades. So if our identity is based on that, it's very fleeting, because it's circumstantial. If you're in a prestigious school where everyone scores really well, and if your source of security and your identity as a person comes from comparison, it makes it very unstable.

Secondly, friendship issues. A lot of youths are still learning how to make friends, and sometimes I have heard of youths who self-harm due to friendship issues. Actually, I know some parents may not fully agree with this, and I also get where they're coming from. Some parents may say things like 'oh these are just friends, you don't need to care about them'. As an adult we can do that, but for a child it can be difficult. They're still learning that. It's not something that they can just give up on immediately.

The last thing would be bullying. Bullying is really terrible but it's happening to many youths. Many of them grow up feeling very unsafe, they feel like they can't trust people, they often feel very traumatized as well, and as a result it causes them to feel suicidal, feeling like people hate them.

Si Qi

I have a bit of a tricky question. Not sure how to phrase it, but these youths we're talking about, they're only, what, fifteen or sixteen? They're only fifteen years old, yet they're bullies, they're shaming their friends for their body image. I'm just wondering, where do they pick up all these things, and why does this happen among youths?

Peggy

I think a contributing factor is the internet. Youths may think *oh it's really cool to talk this way*, or *because it's on the internet I can hide behind a certain facade and not experience any consequences*. Which to some extent, yeah, if they're not being reported, they may not experience any consequences, but other people are experiencing the consequences like emotional issues and feeling anxious.

Si Qi

How can they navigate this cyberspace? It's really hard!

Peggy

Yeah, it is. I think first it is for them to really recognize that the cyberspace is no different from physical interactions. If you are saying something mean to the person, it would still hurt the person's feelings, whether it is online or face to face. Just because you can't see the person's response, it doesn't mean that they're not hurt. Just because they don't reply to you doesn't mean they are okay with it. But it's very hard for them to see it. So it's very important for youths to learn online etiquette, especially relating to mental health. For example, if they know that their friends have mental health issues, it would be more appropriate not to post anything negative about mental health like saying that 'I hate depressed people, they're so bipolar!' If you say things like that, it may affect your friends even if you may not be referring to them. Online etiquette is very important in creating that safe culture on the internet.

Another thing that's very important also is to not post things that are very triggering. If let's say, a celebrity cut herself, and she took a photo, and she showed it online—we can't stop that from happening. But if you know that you have friends who are struggling with this, don't share that picture because it's very triggering. It's also for them to understand what their intention is for posting something. *Is this for fun? Am I trying to share a message? Who would be affected by my posting?* These are the questions that youths need to think about, to take a more mindful stance before they post or write anything that could hurt somebody.

CONNECTING THE DOTS IN YOUR LIFE

Si Qi

Okay, so mental health is a multifaceted issue, right? There are so many factors that come into the picture. You mentioned family, the lack of understanding between generations about what mental health is, then there's the internet, there's social media, there's school, there are friends. So how can we start to address some of these stigmas?

Peggy

It can start from home. If the family has stigma about mental health or the way that they talk about mental health isn't very nice, the child may pick that up as well. And if the child has been struggling with mental health issues, then he or she would feel that it's not safe to approach their parents about mental health issues. And with that, I also want to acknowledge the cultural difference between mental health literacy thirty years ago and now. I think for parents to cope with that, something that they could just do within their own time is for them to think about how mental health relates with them. It is for them to reflect and look back on their lives to see if there were times when they felt their mental health wasn't so good. If they can reflect and have that awareness, it's easier for them to empathize and resonate with their kids. I think many times a lot of families are not in touch with their emotions because they grew up thinking that that's not what they're supposed to do. They're supposed to just ignore it, or just carry on with life.

Si Qi

A big contributing factor to mental health issues is also the lack of emotional connection we have with ourselves, the lack of compassion we have for ourselves, the lack of empathy that we have for ourselves and therefore can't have for others. But what does it mean to connect with ourselves and how do we do it?

Peggy

I would say it's really being able to observe your thoughts and emotions without judging yourself. Without questioning yourself whether you're supposed to feel that way or not. Instead, we can try to take a curious stance towards why you're feeling that way and why you're having those thoughts. Because there is a narrative behind every thought and every emotion, and if we dig deep enough, it will help us understand where some of this comes from. Was it from an experience that we had in the past? How we feel and how we think is often shaped by the experiences we have, and I think it's about being able to connect some of these experiences. Adulthood is not just a phase that is compartmentalized. Adolescence isn't just a phase that is compartmentalized. But how you are as a youth would shape your experiences and how you cope with adulthood, which is why a lot of times if mental health issues are not treated in adolescence, they may pose more challenging problems in adulthood.

On that note about connecting with ourselves, I think mindfulness is something that really helps. Having full awareness of what we're thinking, what's going through our mind, even our body sensations without judging ourselves and just noticing it, connecting ourselves to the present moment will really help us to gain clarity. So that when your kids share with you what they're feeling in the present moment, you can then transfer that skill to them and help them to notice why they're doing that and you may never know, one day your kids may find that answer and share that with you. And through that you might be closer to your kids as well.

Si Qi

And that's why the role of parents and the family is really important. Kids learn everything from the family, both the good and the bad. Okay so last question, if you had a message you would like to share with readers about mental health, what would it be?

Peggy

My message is, if you don't see it, it doesn't mean that it's not there.

CHAPTER 4

We Don't Want To Suffer In Silence

By Muhammad Syazan Bin Saad and Hannah Bastrisyia, Peer Supporters, Temasek Polytechnic

As they both struggled with their mental health, Syazan and Hannah became peer supporters to encourage those also struggling with mental health to reach out for help. They shared the challenges they face at home, work, and the stigmatising reactions from their peers when they talk about their mental health. They hope that people develop a deeper understanding of mental health conditions and how it affects those living with it, instead of forming stereotypes or labels that only serve to alienate them or worsen their condition.

YOU'LL GROW OUT OF IT, IT'S JUST A PHASE

Si Qi

First of all, thank you for doing this interview on Good Friday. I want to find out more from you guys. What made you decide to want to do something in the mental health space? Either Syazan or Hannah can start first.

Syazan

Mental health has been an important topic in my life. Having experienced it personally, I can see first-hand how people are not receptive to this topic. Especially in the Asian culture, we don't see mental illness as a form of real illness per se. Oftentimes in our Asian context, you are seen to have a lack of faith, lack of belief in God, and to solve this you just have to pray more. So over the years, I've been taking the initiative to organise and lead mental health initiatives in school and outside school to help to create this safe space for conversations about mental illness for the student body and for people suffering from mental illnesses.

Hannah

Honestly, it started with a passion to serve. I wanted to find out ways to support the community and I noticed that the mental health community is not really supported in Singapore. A lot of organizations and efforts are not really known, so I wanted to bridge that gap, and being a peer supporter allows me to do that by raising awareness of all these efforts. And also, my personal struggles in mental health gave me more motivation to help those that are suffering as well so that I can help to be their voice.

Si Qi

What was the mental health struggle that you personally went through?

Syazan

I struggled a lot with depression and anxiety. So oftentimes, there's this rollercoaster of emotions and intrusive thoughts that happens. And you just can't help it because it occurs in your daily life. And when you go out of the house, you have to put on an alter ego or a—

Si Qi

Like a mask.

Syazan

A mask. You have to mask the entire issue. It's a lot of personal struggle because it is hard to explain to people if they don't experience it themselves. People are often dismissive about it and they don't know how to support people with mental illnesses.

Si Qi

Why do you feel that you have to put on this mask when you go outside?

Syazan

It's tiring to explain to people what you're going through when they dismiss it every single time. So it just gets to a point they'll ask 'Are you okay?' I'll just say 'Oh yeah, I'm fine, it's nothing'. There's no point explaining anymore if people aren't going to care and are just asking for the sake of asking, not knowing how to respect you for it.

Hannah

I struggled with depression and slight PTSD[7] as well from trauma. I agree with what Syazan said. I get intrusive thoughts, and you

[7] PTSD: Post-Traumatic Stress Disorder

have to put on a very well-thought-out facade so people see it. Because nowadays, people think that it's just a trend. Every time you try to say that you have depression, people will just ask 'Is it a phase?' I don't think sixteen years of my life is a phase! But it starts to become really hard to find someone to talk to who will genuinely validate your feelings. We don't expect to be babied. We just want to be accepted and acknowledged. The fact that we have to keep it a secret when going for job interviews, because the stigma is so real that we have a choice to not disclose it at work, shows how much we have to put up a tough front just to be accepted.

Si Qi

I can totally relate with the need to put on a mask or facade just to survive and function in society. So I want to just go a little bit deeper into this. Can you share with me the mental health stigmas that you have personally experienced?

Syazan

I usually portray myself as a happy-go-lucky person. Someone who smiles and laughs a lot in front of others. So it is hard for people to believe that I'm suffering from depression. Like 'Oh, you're just faking it. You always smile, you always laugh. How could you be depressed?' And that's such a lie. It hurts internally lah, because I think people don't understand that you need to put on this facade in order to survive in the real world, just to be a normal human.

I think at the same time, for something like anxiety, people don't understand the triggers that cause it. It may seem so trivial to the people out there, but because of the experiences you've gone through, it hits you harder. For me, simple things like talking to male counterparts is difficult because growing up, I have a lot of negative experiences being bullied, being physically and mentally hurt, so people just don't understand that these are real lived experiences and not made-up thoughts. I don't appreciate when people just dismiss your claims and say 'You'll grow out of it, it's just a phase, or not everyone is going to attack you in this way'.

Hannah

As for me, I always get the comment that 'You're fine, you're perfectly fine, it's just in your head'. And I mean yes, it's clearly in my head, that's why it's a mental issue, right? I get comments that belittle the trauma that I experienced. As Syazan said, people will say 'Oh, they won't hurt you again'. I know not everyone is going to hurt me, and I don't have to be scared of everyone, but it's just that one experience that occurred for such a long time. It was enough to stick in your head.

As much as young people think *we're so open minded, and we can accept those with mental illnesses*, it's actually not really true. Because right now, it's become so common that it's become a trend, and people start to belittle the symptoms of depression. People associate depression as *oh you're just sad, that's it.* They don't treat it seriously. I'm not expecting people to tiptoe around the topic, but at least validate that it is a real thing and respect that it is an issue that people go through.

The lack of seriousness in the younger community, and the lack of acceptance in the older community, that's the issue.

Si Qi

Right. I'm in my mid-20s, so I'm at least one generation above you guys. I was always under the impression that the younger generations are more open to talking about mental health.

Syazan

I think this topic has become open as it's talked about more in the Gen Z community, but the thing is, when you're more open, you tend to minimise the symptoms too. You don't understand exactly what these symptoms are in order to qualify as a mental illness. So whenever someone is sad for a period of time, they take it to be *I was sad for three days, that means I have depression.* It reduces the severity of the issue. While people are more aware of mental illnesses, people are not conversant enough to understand the severity of it.

Si Qi

I see. So the problem is manifested in a different way, that although people are more aware of these terms, it is perhaps being used very loosely, so people take it quite lightly.

BEING A BRIDGE BETWEEN YOUTHS AND PROFESSIONAL SUPPORT

Si Qi

Could you tell me more about the work that you guys do as peer supporters? What made you decide to go into it?

Syazan

I think me and Hannah entered peer support at the same time. We stumbled upon this support training workshop and we felt that it was really important to support your peers. I think it's reminiscent of physical first aid. As much as you can treat, for example, a burn, it's also very important to support someone who has suicidal ideation. How do you support them through it and in a sense, try to stop them? So over the years, we have been starting various initiatives and volunteering at mental health events to spread the message that mental health illnesses should be taken seriously. At the same time, we should not view these people as different because we're all human beings at the end of the day.

I think regardless of the struggles we go through, we shouldn't be treated differently. So please *please* don't alienate us. We're one of you—we're just suffering from mental illnesses.

Hannah

I want to be that person that they can relate to and they can share what they're going through with. As a peer supporter, you don't solve their issues. You just act as a listening ear, like a friend. You validate their feelings, you support them, and if they need immediate help, we can quickly refer them to the appropriate organizations and people.

A lot of people think that peer supporters solve issues. We don't. We're not counsellors. We're the bridge between counsellors and youths that are troubled, because it's very hard for youths to directly approach counsellors. Maybe they're scared of counsellors and all these confidentiality issues. Sometimes they might even just need someone to talk to get the motivation to go get professional help. That's where we step in.

THE ROLE OF FAMILY, RELIGION AND COMMUNITY IN MENTAL HEALTH

Si Qi

Nice. So, on the topic of seeking help, I'd like to discuss stigmas a bit more. Stigmas are what prevent somebody from stepping forward to get help. So I'm not sure if you guys have seen a counsellor or are seeing one, but what are the stigmas you've faced in your mental health journey?

Syazan

I think I'll answer first. For me, even though I'm a peer supporter, it's difficult for me to even see a counsellor. I think it stems from an internal sense of discrimination. My family isn't very open to talking about mental illnesses, and when they first heard about me from the doctor, they were really shocked. As I mentioned earlier, they'll attribute this to a lack of religious knowledge, lack of prayers, lack of faith. So because it has been so difficult for me, I don't want others to suffer the same way. That's why I want to create a safe space through our peer support initiatives. In our recent event, we advocated the different places people can seek help from—be it helplines, mental health chatbots, and even encouraged them to consider booking an appointment with the counsellor.

Si Qi

Did you go to a school counsellor or an external one?

Syazan

External.

Si Qi

Right, and you went by yourself?

Syazan

Actually, I went with my mum, but it didn't turn out well.
[Syazan laughs]

Si Qi

Ah, okay. Are you still seeing anyone at the moment?

Syazan

Unfortunately, no. So my plan is to wait until I'm twenty-one when I have the authority to make my own medical decisions. I think it is important to note that this is the unfortunate case for many youths in Singapore, where parental authority becomes an impediment to seeking help from mental health professionals, where we technically cannot take control of our own health, and in this case, of our own mental health.

Si Qi

I see. What about you, Hannah?

Hannah

As for me, I'm not professionally diagnosed because my family just thinks that I'm okay with it and I just need to get closer to God. But of course, when I turn twenty-one, I'm going to go, because I know what's wrong with me. But in the meantime, before I get professionally diagnosed, I am undergoing intensive therapy with a therapist every week or every once in two weeks. That's how I'm coping with it at the moment. Because if I were to just wait until I turn twenty-one, I cannot lah, I cannot stabilise myself. I'll be very *very* temperamental, and I don't want to affect the people around me, especially as a peer supporter.

I'm much more emotional than Syazan, so I struggle to control my emotions. I need to speak to someone professional and I need to be able to stabilise myself. I'm slowly trying to get my parents to open up to the idea of me getting diagnosed because it might be very beneficial for me in the future.

Si Qi

I think in the Asian context, family plays a huge part in our lives. It does create more layers of relational dynamics that come into play when somebody wants to seek help or talk about something. What is the role that your family plays in your mental health?

Hannah

That's a good question. I'll go first. For my family, they mean well. I understand where they're coming from, but they're just worried that I won't have a career in the future because of my mental health issues. They're just scared. They will tell me that I need to *get closer to God and you'll be fine,* but that's not the case for me.

Sometimes I just want them to be more accepting about it. It's good that they're supporting me going for therapy lah, but it does get lonely sometimes when your family is shrugging it off. I know that they care for me, but it does get lonely when they don't acknowledge that you're suffering from something. It's not everyone—my siblings do acknowledge that I'm suffering from something. They're just afraid that I won't be able to get a job, and that's fair—it's not really known that you can choose not to disclose your mental illness today, but sometimes I do get very lonely at home.

Syazan

For me, my family embodies more traditional values, so mental illness is one of the taboo topics. For example, when my parents first heard about it from the doctor, they were really shocked. You would expect to receive some emotional support going through tough times, but the opposite happened. I was scolded for it. There's this notion that you can't have a mental illness if you're not crazy enough to be mentally ill. They have this perception that everyone in IMH[8] is psychotic, can't handle themselves, or are mentally incapable of making decisions and the like. So you're just not seen as suffering that badly compared to others. But in reality, everyone suffers differently from various types of mental illnesses, and I think in the Asian community, it's not well understood. People need to understand that mental illnesses extend beyond psychosis, such as mood and anxiety disorders, and they deserve the right to seek treatment without judgment. However, these topics are swept under the rug and if anything happens, you're supposed to deal with it yourself.

Si Qi

---

[8] IMH: Institute of Mental Health (Singapore's only hospital dedicated to mental health)

Could you share more about the relationship between your mental health and religion?

Hannah

Syazan and I are Muslim. For us, there's always that stigma where if you're having a mental illness, you're not holy enough. You're not close to God enough, the devil is in you, that kind of thing. But we need to validate mental health issues in the religious setting. Even mosques and other religious organizations have therapy and counselling for those who are not comfortable speaking to a secular counsellor and want to seek something within their religion.

But people don't really see that actually, religion accepts people like this too. I feel that they just need to be more open minded about this topic.

The therapy and counselling sessions that religious organizations offer are not mass prayers. They just take an Islamic lens in the sessions. For instance, in Islam, we value patience, so they impart the values of being patient with yourself and you having the patience to get better—these types of principles that are also related to religion.

If someone were to have a physical illness or injury—say they broke their leg—people wouldn't say 'You're not holy enough, that's why you broke your leg'. They'll probably say 'Oh, it happened for a reason'.

Syazan

There was a point in time when I was a little confused. Is it really true that when your elders tell you that when you're suffering from a mental illness, it means you're lacking faith? It reached a point in time when I reached out to my religious teachers in the mosque, who happened to be working in IMH, to find out from a scholar's perspective. And I learned that mental illnesses are actually not discriminated in Islam.

Si Qi

Thank you for sharing that.

So, you guys have shared a little bit about the ways in which you will want to address mental health stigmas, and in fact, you are already doing it through the peer support group. Is there anything else you hope to see happen in your community or the society to address mental health stigmas?

Syazan

I've been doing more campus-based projects. For example, I have organised a long-term project collaboration with the Singapore Association of Mental Health to help volunteers and persons with mental illnesses interact and create a safe space for conversation. I hope that people will understand that there's nothing different about persons with mental illnesses, and it doesn't make you any less human.

In terms of community, say the Malay community, I do acknowledge that there are movements out there by various community organizations that try to break the stigma and help people understand mental illnesses. In fact, it has been spoken about during Friday prayers. But I think in order for this to have a better outreach or at least a better understanding, it's not just about people listening and forgetting about it. We need to engage people better. The upcoming fasting month, I think, will be a great time to talk about mental health. The recent pandemic will also help people reflect and understand the impact of it. It will also be helpful for people who have suffered with mental illnesses to talk about it.

In fact, the Malay community is quite talkative. We just like to share and tell people whatever we learnt, whatever we heard.

So I think it helps to take these small but meaningful steps towards this conversation on mental illness.

Hannah

Yeah, I definitely agree with Syazan.

I notice that the older generation will always tie in religion, so we can look into working together with religious organizations to bring awareness of mental health into the community.

We also have to work with families to bring that awareness and knowledge to parents. That's not to say that your kid will definitely have something wrong with them, but we can prepare young parents or parents-to-be to understand that mental struggles are a real thing, and how parents can accept and grow with their children rather than discriminate against them.

If we were to have supportive families and religious communities, I feel that society would be much better at tackling mental illnesses and accepting and validating those with mental illnesses. In a sense, Syazan and I don't have to hide our suffering from others.

Si Qi

There are many areas that need to come together to tackle this issue, right?

Hannah

Yeah. I feel our schools are doing enough. Because schools are pumping out a lot of awareness for this issue.

Si Qi

What kind of support do you guys have at school?

Hannah

The peer support movement is one. I notice schools are having more mental health, mental wellness talks now. In primary schools, I used to have to go to the counsellor once a semester or once in a few weeks to get checked on.

Si Qi

Really?

Hannah

It's compulsory. We have people who will think it's just a session for some activities but lowkey, the counsellor is just assessing us. In secondary school I had a lot of wellness talks. And we got more of that during O Levels. I feel like the school was just watching from afar to catch students from spiraling down during that stressful period.

Si Qi

Wow! Did you have that in your school, Syazan?

Syazan

I wouldn't say that I had the same experience, actually. I think the majority of the mental health talks that I'm aware of were in Polytechnic. So there's this inter-IHL movement that speaks on the topic of mental health. And there are a lot of talks in school, and the introduction of the WYSA chatbot—

Si Qi

What is WYSA?

Syazan

It's this mobile app that students can use to speak their mind on mental illnesses, and they can actually book an appointment with a counsellor within the app itself. I think that's a really innovative solution for people who are not comfortable with seeking and talking to an actual counsellor.

In my opinion, I think while schools are talking about mental health, more needs to be done to reach the older generations, even on a national scale. I wrote about this in one of my essays. I was basically saying that schools have been talking about mental health, but what about workplaces? I don't really see this being spoken about.

For example, when I did my internship, I spoke to my supervisor at the end of the internship about my struggles. She shared with me that 'In this sector, people don't really talk about mental health because people will have certain perceptions of you, so it's better to just keep it to yourself because you don't want others to see you as vulnerable, as someone who can't handle themselves'. So I hope that adults and youths can come together to create an open and safe community where all of us come together to understand mental health.

YOU'RE NOT ALONE

Si Qi

If there are any last words you would want to leave the readers with about mental health, what would they be?

Hannah

You're not alone. That's very important because most of the time, people that suffer from this feel very, very, very alone. So if there's one thing I would like to let these people that are suffering like us know is that you are not alone. We are here together, we are one community, we are here for each other.

Syazan

Speak to someone, whoever may be. Be it your parents, friends, or even teachers—whoever you're comfortable with. I think speaking to someone helps to open this first step. If people know that you're struggling, at least you know that you can rely on them if anything happens.

CHAPTER 5

Supporting Every Child and Youth's Mental Health

By Cayden Woo, Deputy Director, Sunbeam Place @ Children's Society and Jeremy Heng, Clinical Psychologist, SSF-R @ Children's Society

Cayden and Jeremy's work involves supporting children with adverse childhood experiences. These children are often at risk of developing mental health conditions, or falling into a pattern of crime as well because of what they witnessed and experienced growing up. In their journey to support these children, Cayden and Jeremy both stress the importance of incorporating mental health structures and emotional literacy into a child's environment and upbringing.

LENDING A VOICE FOR VULNERABLE CHILDREN

Si Qi

So what made you guys decide to embark on this career?

Jeremy

I'm a psychologist by training, and I support the children and young person's home (CYPH) at Sunbeam Place and the reunification team. For me, I think it would be my faith as well as my previous volunteering experience. I was working with a few disadvantaged families by volunteering as a tutor, and at the Meet-the-People sessions. In my previous role as a research assistant, I was working with families from different SES[9] levels. And you could already see, even for children aged two from lower SES families, the impact it had on their development.

So when I was volunteering for example, I felt that I was supporting children in terms of their academics, but I couldn't help them in terms of gaining skills like social or emotion regulation to help them to get out of that cycle. That's why I pursued further studies in psychology.

Cayden

Since I graduated, I've been working with different populations in social services. I was doing prison aftercare work, and I was doing family service center work. During the course of my work, I saw how when parents are incarcerated, when families are experiencing conflicts at home dealing with the stressors in life, it is the children who experience the largest impact. So that really sparked the interest in me to want to work with children to support their mental health. That's why I came into the children's homes sector and I've worked in different children's

[9] SES: Socioeconomic status

homes for almost nine years already. I feel that it's very rewarding, seeing how we can protect them, lend them a voice, support them and reunify them with their family or even back to society.

Si Qi

I think one common misconception about children and mental health is this idea that they are like oil and water. They don't seem to match. People are like, 'Wait children got mental health issues meh? How can that be, they should be happy and carefree.' So there's that kind of stigma and misconception in society. From your experience, what are some of the challenges that kids face in terms of mental health?

Jeremy

First of all, I want to say this—mental health is not a dirty word. Mental health is like physical health. It is a continuum where you can have positive mental health, you can have times where your mental health is just okay, and you can have times when your mental health deteriorates to the point where you're no longer functioning, and that's when mental health disorders can happen. So if we can have that kind of understanding for physical health, that a child can have a cough, but they can also have something as serious as fever and COVID and cancer so on, then the same goes for mental health as well. Children can experience mental health concerns when the culture and environment that they're in doesn't support their functioning and instead promotes the development of mental health concerns. That is a possibility.

And, like Cayden mentioned, in the population that we work with, children experience many more adverse childhood experiences (ACEs) and the likelihood of experiencing mental health concerns significantly increases.[10] This manifests in

[10] Liu, Denise, Chi Meng Chu, Lee Hong Neo, Rebecca P. Ang, Michelle Yan Ling Tan, and Jeanie Chu, 'Multiple Trauma Exposure And Psychosocial Functioning

different forms, such as depression, anxiety disorders and self-harm[11], which has been escalating in the recent years, so that would be the challenge that we're dealing with.

Si Qi

What are the most common mental health conditions that you see in children today?

Jeremy

I don't think we have a national study for children but the top three disorders among adults are major depressive disorder, alcohol abuse and obsessive-compulsive disorder.[12]

Some of the key ones we're seeing in the children and youth in the Out-of-Home Care setting are mood related issues. Trauma is very prevalent in our population too. Self-harming, at risk behaviours. So things like the likelihood of committing offences, violence, aggression, are some of the things we are dealing with in this population and again I don't have the statistics on hand but if you look up MSF-published[13] research[14], we do see that a higher proportion of juvenile offenders have a history of being

---

In Singaporean Children In Out-Of-Home Care.', Psychological Trauma: Theory, Research, Practice, And Policy, 2016, 8 (4): 431-438. doi:10.1037/tra0000098

[11] Kim Ho, 'A Third Of Singaporeans Have Experienced Suicidal Thoughts', Yougov: What The World Thinks, 2019. https://sg.yougov.com/en-sg/news/2019/06/25/sg-mentalhealth-selfharm/

[12] Subramaniam, M., E. Abdin, J. A. Vaingankar, S. Shafie, B. Y. Chua, R. Sambasivam, Y. J. Zhang, et al., 'Tracking the Mental Health of a Nation: Prevalence and Correlates of Mental Disorders in the Second Singapore Mental Health Study', Epidemiology and Psychiatric Sciences 29, 2020: e29. doi:10.1017/S2045796019000179

[13] MSF: Ministry of Social and Family Development

[14] Chu Chi Meng, Stuart D. M. Thomas, and Vivienne P. Y. Ng, 'Childhood Abuse And Delinquency: A Descriptive Study Of Institutionalized Female Youth In Singapore', Psychiatry, Psychology And Law, 2009, 16 (sup1): S64-S73. doi:10.1080/13218710802552971

abused or experiencing adverse childhood experiences, which is consistent with international trends. So we can see that generally the odds are against the individual.

Cayden

I feel that a lot of times when we talk about mental health related to children and youth, often the notion of mental health is really from an adult lens.

Children think differently from adults and they experience the world differently from grown-ups. I think what's currently lacking, not just in Singapore but worldwide, is in trying to see mental health from the children's lens, because to them, depression and anxiety are very different from how adults term it. Disruptions in their sleep, schoolwork, or in building relationships can be very similar to depressive symptoms for children but it might not be diagnosed as depression. We really need to step into children's ways of knowing and doing to be able to understand when things are not right for them. We may underestimate the severity of what children are experiencing if we look at it from an adult's perspective, when in reality it is worth our concern, worth adults lending supportive hands and listening ears. So I feel that there might be a small gap of understanding children's mental health. If the child is not clinically diagnosed, then there might not be much support for them. But it should be equally concerning. Children's positive mental health starts with the adults around them. As adults, we need to help them feel safe and help them make sense of their feelings.

Si Qi

So right now there isn't a set of clinical diagnosis for children for depression? Or is it the same diagnosis for both adults and children?

Cayden

This, one must ask the psychologist.
[laughter]

Jeremy

The symptoms and criteria of clinical mental health disorders are largely guided by two bodies of guidelines—the Diagnostic and Statistical Manual of Mental Disorders 5th Edition (DSM-5) from the American Psychological Association (APA), and the International Classification of Diseases 11th Edition (ICD-11) from the World Health Organization (WHO). The criteria is largely the same for both adults and children, but the guidelines also account for how the manifestation of certain behaviours may vary according to developmental stages. So for clinicians in hospitals, polyclinics, and practitioners like ourselves, these are the guidelines that shape our assessment and intervention processes. But we note that guidelines may change over time. How our children and youths present themselves is always changing.

Si Qi

That's very true.

Jeremy

I don't think there can ever be a guideline for mental health the same way as how we can have one for other physical conditions. I don't think—correct me if I'm wrong—but when we were younger, I don't think self-harm was as prevalent and we see that coming up a little bit more today. But is that a symptom of internal experiences manifesting differently in this day and age? I think that's a possibility.

INTERNET CULTURE, CYBERBULLYING AND MENTAL HEALTH

Si QI

Yeah, I think that's a lot to think about, that mental health issues manifest very differently compared to physical health, and it changes across generations and is hard to track. Do you think it's related to culture as well? Like internet culture for the kids today especially?

Jeremy

I wouldn't say definitely but I would think it's a high possibility. Youth these days have social media, and they have different kinds of online material, and when they see something they can relate to and they model it, that's one pathway of how a symptom can manifest. Another thing with social media is that it's so multifaceted that I think adults can't really track it too. For example, we just learned that there are 'spam accounts', 'public' accounts and 'private' accounts on multiple platforms such as Twitter, Instagram, Facebook, and TikTok. Children and youths use those platforms to express how they feel and the pain that they experience, but for our generation we didn't have these many platforms.

Cayden

In fact, cyber wellness is very linked to mental wellness, and mental wellness is very different from mental illness. I think this is something we have to debunk as well. Because mental illness and mental wellness are different. Mental illness is where you're diagnosed with a mental disorder by a psychiatrist. The youth today use it very loosely, *oh I'm very depressed, I'm having depression, I'm having anxiety issues.* But their anxiety levels may not be meeting that threshold of a clinical diagnosis, so it's not really to the extent of a mental illness. So then the focus is back on mental wellness. How can we help them to understand their mental wellness and mental wellbeing? How can we help them understand the different possible disorders or some of the ways they can cope better with their academic stress, relationships, and an ever-changing cyberspace? Hence, it is important to mend our youths' mental wellbeing in an online world. Because of the Fear of Missing Out (FOMO) syndrome, I think they don't want to miss out, they don't want to be isolated, and that can create a lot of stress in their mental wellbeing if they're not able to manage it well.

Si Qi

So on the topic of cyber wellness right, we can zoom into cyberbullying as well. I think that's a major issue that kids today face. Could you tell us a bit more about the cyberbullying trends that you see and what effects it has on the kids? And how should we deal with it?

Cayden

Okay so maybe I can differentiate the mainstream children and vulnerable children. Mainstream children are children from the general public. So they are often stressed about their academics. *Can I get into the IP*[15] *schools? Can I get good grades? Can I meet my parents' expectations? Can I be a part of the cool clique of friends?* Some of their parents might come from a higher-SES and they might be more attuned in teaching their kids how to navigate the cyberspace. However, some parents might not have time to teach their kids and would often rely on the schools to do that.

Shifting our focus to vulnerable children, this is where they will have different sets of issues. For example, children in children's homes do not have as much contact with their parents as mainstream children as they are in the children's home most of the time. So the staff in the children's home would have to spend time to help them navigate this space. Many of them want to be connected with their friends even more as they don't want to feel left out, so they invest even more time on social media. Without proper guidance, they'll get lost very easily. And then all

[15] IP: Integrated Programme

this cyberbullying comes like *you're from a poor family, you're stupid, you don't get good grades, you don't belong to our cliques.* All these remarks start to come into their cyberspace.

Jeremy

I'm going to add on to some of the things that Cayden has elaborated on. I think I would say that to some degree—and I'm no means an expert in this area—there are some similarities between physical bullying and cyberbullying. We are all social beings who want to be accepted. When you're physically bullying someone, you're essentially telling them that 'You're not as good as me and I'm rejecting you'. I think cyberbullying to some degree has that element as well. You feel rejected, you feel put down and you feel the shame. Moreover, whatever is posted online stays online forever, and other people can come in to add oil to the flame. So those are some key difficulties in addressing cyberbullying.

Besides the fact that cyberbullying stays online forever, that everyone gets to see it and it's magnified, I think adults these days are not as savvy in stopping that bullying. If it's in school or if it's physical, you can tell the person who was bullied to ignore or to walk away, or we can address the bully. But these days with online trolls, fake accounts who are likely to be bolder because of anonymity, it's so hard to hold someone accountable. And like what Cayden mentioned, for our youth these days, the social world is their world. You can't ask them to be disconnected and ignore that. So when they go into their cyberspace and the bullying is still there, then what? I think that would be the challenge that our youths today experience.

And to add even more layers of complexity, I think as adults our brains have matured so we know when to step back because we know our warning signs. But our children and youths, whose brains and decision-making capabilities are in the process of developing, are more likely to just go with what's on trend and with how they feel. This makes it really hard to protect them, so it's a challenge to protect our youths these days.

THE IMPORTANCE OF A SAFE AND SUPPORTIVE HOME ENVIRONMENT

Si Qi

I want to understand a little more about vulnerable children. So you mentioned earlier on that you could see the impacts of being in a vulnerable family situation for children as young as two years old. What is the youngest child that you guys came into contact with?

Cayden

For Sunbeam Place, so far, the youngest child that's come to us is maybe seven to eight years old.

Si Qi

Before that?

Cayden

Before that they are usually put up for fostering or adoption because they are younger, so the chances of them being fostered or adopted is higher.

Si Qi

Right. So could you give us more details—what is the link between family conflict, family issues or financial stresses that the parents are facing, and the mental health of children?

Cayden

So I think the impact would definitely be greater especially when they're younger because their brains are developing under such stressful stimulation, where their parents are often fighting, always trying to find food and shelter. Under such a stressful environment, they are always in fight or flight mode. Experiencing all these stressors while their brains are still developing will definitely have an impact on their mental wellbeing. This would impact how they function in their social relationships, in their academics and things like that.

Si Qi

You know, sometimes you will hear aunties or uncles talk about the child in front of the child and say things like 'Aiyah, he doesn't understand one', as if the child doesn't know what the adults are talking about. So how do the children actually process the information that there is conflict and instability in their environment?

Cayden

I think it's back to whether the child or youth has that level of safety and attunement with adults. Because you can receive a lot of nasty remarks outside, but if you know that your parents are still there for you when you go home, you know your parents are attuned to you, you know that you are safe at home with the adults that you're with, you bounce back faster. But if you receive all these remarks and you know that nobody supports you back home, your parents don't care about you, you don't feel a sense of safety with the adults you're with, and you have no attunement with other people, then it will be really difficult.

Another point I would like to bring up is that people have a certain amount of resilience. So resilience is another very important factor in counterbalancing your adversity. Some children might not receive a lot of support from others, but if the child is just very resilient, he or she can just bounce back with all these adverse childhood experiences.

Jeremy

I'm going to talk about two concepts, I'm going to be a little technical about it so if you have any questions . . .

Si Qi

Yes, I think it's good to be technical here!

Jeremy

First would be the idea of attachment. Cayden has mentioned a bit about it. The idea of attachment is the quality of the emotional bond that a child and the primary caregiver or the main caregivers would have. In simple terms, secure attachment is where one has a positive view of self and others and is more likely to be related to healthier life outcomes; while insecure attachment relates to a negative view of self and others and is less likely to be related to healthy life outcomes, although it is very much still possible. And this mental lens that you developed when you were really young, in the first three years of your life, impacts how you continue to negotiate with the social world around you, in preschool, in kindergarten, in primary school so on and so forth. You can imagine the cumulative effects of the impact of the quality of attachment over time. For instance, if you have an insecure attachment, you're more likely to have challenges in social interactions with other children. It could make it difficult for you to relate to your teachers and learn well in school, and you get labelled. The repercussions accumulate as you progress through the developmental years. What we know from research is that how sensitive, attuned, and available a caregiver is to an infant in the early years, as early as three to six months, has an impact on the type of attachment the child will have, which in turn affects all these other areas—socioemotional, language, and cognitive outcomes.

Si Qi

Wow, three to six months?

Jeremy

Yes, which is why I think our government, with the understanding from the latest research literature, recognizes that ages zero to three is a really sensitive and critical period of development and for intervention. If you were to look at some of the initiatives by the government, there are two major ways they have stepped in. Firstly, they have piloted the KidSTART programme about five years ago[16], and they found that it's important and helpful to support mothers and their unborn children. So if there is a pregnant mother who fits the criteria for the programme, they'll go in to start supporting the family with social intervention to make sure that the mother is eating right, teach her parenting skills, and help the family stabilize. The programme continues to support the family when the child is born all the way till age six. Currently, any children under age six from disadvantaged families are eligible for the programme. Singapore Children's Society was recently appointed in November 2020 as one of the KidSTART agencies to support this effort. Secondly, in recent years, the preschool education sector has grown in importance, undergone regulation, received significant investments, and has been increasingly made accessible. The government is coming in to make sure that we have quality education, and it starts from preschool because the early years are really crucial.

I think the second concept is the idea of development. Briefly, our brain is made up of three main parts. There's the brain stem, which is the most primitive part that regulates our sleep, breathing, all the basic functions. Then there's the middle portion known as the limbic system which is more involved in emotional regulation and memory, and then there's the top and frontal parts of our brain which is involved in higher-

[16] Early Childhood Development Agency, 'Fact Sheet On KidSTART Visitation,' March 8, 2017, https://www.ecda.gov.sg/PressReleases/Pages/FACT-SHEET-ON-KIDSTART-HOME-VISITATION.aspx

order cognitive processing. For instance, self-control, language, planning, and decision-making. During the early stages of life, the development of our brain is hierarchical. The brain stem develops first, followed by the development of the limbic system. As we mature even further, the top and frontal parts known as the cortex and neocortex of our brain then develop. When a child is placed in an environment where there are a lot of adverse childhood experiences, there's poverty, there's not enough nutrition, insufficient cognitive stimulation, parents are fighting, lack of emotional warmth from caregivers, caregiver is abusive, what then happens is that the development of the limbic system, cortex and neocortex under intense and prolonged stress would be compromised. This means that a child with more ACEs is likely to be at a disadvantage in areas of emotional regulation, stress management and higher-order cognitive processing compared to children who have had healthy environments to grow up in. That's how we may understand how early life experiences may influence the trajectory of development at a neurocognitive level.[17]

Si Qi

Wow. Those are huge impacts.

INTERVENTION APPROACHES FOR VULNERABLE CHILDREN AND YOUTHS

Si Qi

What is the intervention like for these children? I guess we can focus on Sunbeam Place. How do you guys support them?

---

[17] Julia I. Herzog and Christian Schmahl, 'Adverse Childhood Experiences And The Consequences On Neurobiological, Psychosocial, And Somatic Conditions Across The Lifespan', Front Psychiatry, 2019, 9:420. doi:10.3389/fpsyt.2018.00420

Cayden

It will definitely be a multidisciplinary approach where we have social workers, psychologists, care staff, education staff, to come together hand in hand to look at a holistic development for every child. For example, in social-emotional wellbeing, social workers and psychologists will work together very closely. Let's say when a child first comes in, our psychologist will do an intake assessment to see whether the child has any possible trauma symptoms or any difficulties. And if so, and the child comes in with PTSD (Post-traumatic Stress Disorder), then we will refer the child for further intervention. For example, one of the gold standards is TD-CBT (Trauma-focused cognitive behavioral therapy). This is one of the intervention approaches we take in terms of supporting children in managing post-traumatic stress disorder. To give you another example, if a child comes in with learning difficulties, then we might bring the child for dyslexic assessment and if assessed to be so, we'll send the child for dyslexia programmes or any other programmes that can help the child to catch up with their peers.

We'll also provide regular counselling, checking in to look at some of the personal narratives they may have constructed. *Why did I come to a children's home? Why are my parents quarrelling but I'm the one who's being sent away?* Counselling helps them untie all these knots and build and repair their relationship with their parents.

Our care staff play a very important role as well. They provide them with mentorship, and often, it is to help them navigate certain issues in life or even to learn independent living skills. Sometimes when we are not with our parents, we might not have the chance to learn how to iron and wash clothes, how to wash shoes and do financial budgeting. So our care staff really have to take up that role to help them to gain all those independent living skills so that they can be independent when they grow up. Our care staff also looks into the behavioural aspect. Often, children don't have a lot of control in their lives when they're with their parents. Their parents are in control of them. So when they're away from their parents, they'll want to have control, so they'll start to break boundaries, disrespect rules, and so on. Our staff plays a very important role in helping them understand their own behaviour and how they can replace some of the undesirable behaviours with more desirable behaviours.

Jeremy

So with timely, early, and sufficient intervention, we're hoping to replace or even rectify what these children didn't get to experience when they were younger. And hopefully, with enough support and the right structure and interventions, we try to put the child or the youth back on track in comparison to the normal population. And hopefully when things are more stable, they can then exit the system. I think that's always our goal. And besides supporting youth, Sunbeam Place also works really closely with the community partners to try to stabilize the family because if the child is stable and then they go back home and the family's not stable then—

Si Qi

It just reverts back.

Jeremy

It just reverts back. That's why we work really closely not only with the youth and their parents to maintain contact, but also with community partners help to stabilize the parents, because the family connection is really important

I'M NOT GOOD ENOUGH, THERE'S SOMETHING WRONG WITH ME

Si Qi

What do you think are some of the mental health stigmas that society has towards children?

Jeremy

I think at the end of the day, a lot of the stigma that comes from the children themselves or from others is that *I'm not good enough.* Or *there's something wrong with me. If I have a problem, then there's something wrong with me and I'm not accepted in my community.* So I would say that in essence that is the stigma that our youths experience amongst their peers.

Si Qi

So it's a personal stigma that they face?

Jeremy

It's both. I think if the community has a stigma against you, then you internalize that stigma about yourself as well. If a youth were to say that 'I have depression and I have anxiety and I have a certain kind of mental health concern', what does the youth want to hear the most? Probably that 'it's okay, let's get you some help, or you're supported, I still love you, I want to protect you, let's try to support you'. What they fear the most is the direct opposite right? *There's something wrong with you, you're faking it*, and that's perceived as rejection and no wonder youths, and even adults these days still find it hard to come forward and get help.

Si Qi

Because you have a problem, therefore you are the problem. So how can you show people that I have a problem and therefore how can you step forward to get help right?

Jeremy

Yeah. It's that idea of how come when I have a problem, what I experience is shame and guilt, and what I get from the people around me is rejection? If I have a cough, or if I have COVID or if I have cancer, I go to someone that I trust and I tell them about my illness. I don't even have to trust the person completely, as long as they're a safe adult or friend who can take me to a doctor, or ask me to see one. But with mental health disorders or concerns, you don't get that kind of support. You feel shame, you feel guilty for burdening the family member, so you'll choose to keep quiet and usually when that happens, the problem intensifies or accumulates.

Cayden

I totally agree with what Jeremy has said. Adding on to that, it is really the need to belong. A lot of times when children don't receive attention from their teachers, from their parents, from their friends, they feel very lonely and isolated. Some of them might resort to self-harm behaviour and over time this might develop into anxiety related issues, depressive related issues. All these behaviours are very superficial, very surface level, and it's really about how we try to empathize with them, understand them, and find out what is underlying these behaviours so that we can resolve the root issues rather than just the surface problems.

Si Qi

And the emotional vocabulary right, we are not taught to feel but we're taught to perform in school, to hit our goals. But we don't learn how to express our sadness or anger in a healthy way, so it just keeps bottling up and one day when you're an adult and you realize you're still dealing with the same thing you were as a teenager or as a child.

FACING TRAUMATIC INCIDENTS IN CHILDHOOD

Si Qi

So I know you mentioned a little bit about PTSD and trauma. I think I want to discuss it a little more. From a professional perspective, what is childhood trauma and why does it still affect adults, even though they are fully grown, fifty, forty-year-old adults?

Jeremy

So I would say . . . Cayden, jump in if I miss something out. Trauma is a stressful event, but it's extremely stressful to the point where it endangers and causes the individual to feel that their life is threatened. It's an extremity of stress. So for example, harsh physical punishments that require medical attention as opposed to maybe a tap on a hand or parents scolding you for a short period of time. If you experienced harsh physical punishment to the point where your life may have been at stake, that may be one form of trauma. Physical abuse, domestic violence, bullying, neglect, sexual assault, separation from caregivers (by death or incarceration) or even witnessing traumatic events experienced by others are some forms of trauma. Other forms of trauma that children and youth may experience could be emotional abuse. So yes, there's no physical wound but the impact on the self-concept of the individual on a cumulative, daily basis, threatens the individual's development of self. People may experience the same incident, but not everyone would go on to have PTSD.

BUILDING RESILIENCE IN OUR GROWING YEARS

Si Qi

You mentioned earlier that resilience is a huge factor in them being able to bounce back. So I think it's a really important concept. Is there a way that youths and children can build that resilience? [short pause]

Si Qi

Is that a difficult question?

Jeremy

It is a difficult question because the idea of operationalizing it has also been really difficult.

Cayden

I think one very important thing that we can teach and pass on to them is coping skills.

How can we help them cope with their emotions better? For example, if I'm dysregulating, I'm very angry, I'm feeling triggered by something, what are some of the coping tools I can use? It could be paying attention to my breathing, counting one to ten, and doing visualizing exercises. All these are very important coping skills and for some children, nobody around them can teach them that. If they can learn all these coping skills and be able to deploy it when they're triggered, it will help them to manage these different stresses in life more effectively.

Jeremy

Of course there'll be trial and error, *maybe this is not good for me, maybe I'll try another coping skill.* So they can try different coping skills until they really find the one that's most effective for them, and that will really help them in the long run.

I think that there would be three other things that could possibly contribute to resilience.

One is sense-making. When you experience failure or hardship, what happens after that? Do you blame yourself and think that there's no point doing this anymore? And do people around you reinforce that idea? Or do you tell yourself that actually *it's okay, yeah failure is really painful and it really hurts but I'll just try it again and do it in a different way, or I'll do it in the same way, but with some adjustments?* So sense-making is something that contributes to resilience a lot. And I think it's a cumulative experience because if you have this kind of mindset, and you reinforce it over the years, it continues throughout your life. In literature, you hear it a lot as growth mindset.[18] That's the first thing.

The second one is whether you have someone who can hold you and support you through the hardships that you experience. In families where there's a safe adult or there's a stable attachment figure that's able to be attuned to you, to support you and hold you through the hardship, you'll know it's okay and you can continue to trust the world and yourself. That is really important to the development of resilience.[19]

The third is the idea of self-efficacy. It is the idea that you believe that what you do and your efforts will result in a positive change. Unfortunately for a lot of the beneficiaries that we meet, they feel that whatever they do is not effective or that there's no point, so they don't do it at all and they just go off track. But if the youth is able to see that what they do has a positive result,

---

[18] David Scott Yeager and Carol S. Dweck, 'Mindsets That Promote Resilience: When Students Believe That Personal Characteristics Can Be Developed'. Educational Psychologist, 2012, 47 (4): 302-314. doi:10.1080/00461520.2012.722805

[19] Toh Sze Min, Charlene Fu, Chan Qing Rong, Fang Xinwei, Nisa Nurdini Binte Johar, 'Do Close Relationships with Caregivers Help Build Children's Resilience to Adversity?', Research Bites, 2019, https://www.childrensociety.org.sg/resources/ck/files/research-bites-issue-8-february-2020.pdf

then they will start to believe in themselves a little bit more, and that contributes to that cumulative effect. So let's take the case of a youth who has come from a difficult family background and is in a lower academic stream in secondary school. If you can develop resilience, if you have someone to support you, to give you additional academic support, to tell you that 'It's okay, you're in this stream but you can continue to push forward', and then you do well in school, you progress and you know that *hey actually if I study hard, I can do well* and then we see that happening for the rest of their lives so that's one way of how resilience can be nurtured.

Si Qi

So for kids who feel that they've hit a wall and there's nowhere else they can go, Tinkle Friend is a helpline they can call. So what is Tinkle Friend and what does it do?

Cayden

So Tinkle Friend[20] is a toll-free helpline all primary school-aged children in Singapore can call, especially in situations when their parents or main caregivers are not available to attend to them. We have trained volunteers and staff who will attend to these children. They can share their concerns and issues anonymously. In 2014, a Tinkle Friend online chat line was introduced.

During the Circuit Breaker[21] period, we experienced a surge in the online chats and a number of children did talk to us about the stress they were facing. This could be academic stress, whether they're able to get into IP schools or DSA[22] schools, getting good

[20] Tinkle Friend: https://www.tinklefriend.sg/

[21] Circuit Breaker refers to the three-month nationwide lockdown in Singapore to curb the spread of COVID-19

[22] DSA: Direct School Admission

results, not meeting parents' expectations, so on and so forth. We had many chats related to these issues, and our staff and trained volunteers help to provide some support, but if the issue gets too complicated then we will see whether we can redirect the child to their respective school counsellors for more in-depth follow-up work.

Jeremy

On top of academic stress and not being able to meet parents' expectations, one of the key stresses during that period, according to my colleagues, was the lack of access to social support, because you stay at home and you can't go to school to meet your friends. The other thing was not being able to meet their friends but having to stay at home with their parents who also have to stay at home because of work, and this created a double tension for them.

IDENTIFYING SOME GAPS WITH REGARDS TO MENTAL HEALTH INTERVENTION FOR CHILDREN

Si Qi

What do you guys think we can do on various levels, from the individual, to family, community, even the national level, to address these mental health stigmas amongst youth and children?

Cayden

I think the emphasis at the national level on the importance of mental wellness is very important because it can have a trickle-down effect where mental health can get recognized at the other levels as well. We can get schools to recognize the importance of mental wellness for students. We can get different community partners and stakeholders to play their role in supporting mental wellness. For example, coming up with programmes that are targeted at each age group or at a certain population to promote things we can do to help ourselves cope with stress better. We can even create awareness at the family level, such as guiding parents to recognize that mental wellness is equally important as academic results, and how parents can play their role in supporting their children. And this effort should be coordinated, not just left up to the individual to see whether it is important for them. So having that national campaign and driving the effort is important, which I feel that we are on the right track. Compared to the past, mental health is now more recognized by society. We are more aware about mental wellbeing and self-care. In the adult world we keep talking about self-care right, but we need to emphasize that message in the children and youth world as well.

Jeremy

For myself, it would be the idea of mental health literacy, having the vocabulary to describe what you're feeling inside. From the 2016 Singapore Mental Health Study[23], one in seven Singaporeans will have a mental health condition in our lifetime, and for that group, there's a delay of about four to eleven years from the onset of the symptoms to getting help, which is unacceptable.[24] The research has suggested two likely barriers for getting help. One is mental health stigma, and the other is not recognizing the symptoms, not knowing where and when to escalate and get help. I think having campaigns and education at the school level would be really important for youths. That's how we can do them justice. It would help the youths and children to know what they're feeling, why they're feeling it, and at which level it is no longer healthy and therefore they should get help. This kind of psychoeducation should transcend to the

[23] IMH, Singapore Mental Health Study (2016)

[24] The study showed that people with OCD had a treatment delay (estimated in median values) of 11 years, followed by a treatment delay of 4 years for people with bipolar disorder and alcohol abuse.

general population because when the children and youth turn to get help, the people whom they turn to for help must also be able to support them because it's not helpful if the youth know that okay, I think there's something wrong, I need to get help but the parents or family members say no lah just don't worry, don't cry, just sleep it'll be okay. That's not helpful.

I would say we probably should look at how we can integrate the mental health services in the sector a little bit better. I think there are a lot of services but as a service user, if you're someone with mental health concerns, where do you start? I don't think that's very clear for members of the public, so I think that's an area we can do a little bit more. We have a lot of campaigns, we know there are a lot of services out there, but when I need the help then what do I do?

Si Qi

It's like do I go to a GP or a polyclinic? Can GP give medication for mental health? Actually, I know they can, but it's not very widely known.

Jeremy

But medication is not—

Si Qi

Yeah that's another thing.

Jeremy

Yeah that's another thing, right? From previous interviews I think you would know that medications address the symptom but doesn't address the core of many mental health issues. For example, for a youth who is bullied and presents with depression and self-harm, antidepressants can help alleviate the mood, but the bullying, the bullies, the impact of bullying, learning to cope, the sense of self, and sense-making all need to be addressed. That's where counselling and psychotherapy is really important and that's an additional layer of concern because who can access these services? I think it's more likely that SES comes into play because for lower-income groups, they may perceive psychological intervention as less necessary compared to their many tasks in day-to-day living, be less certain about where to get help from, and experience reduced accessibility to these services. Individuals in lower-income families also are more likely to have difficulties in attending intervention as regularly. So I think those are the things that we can do more as a sector.

Cayden

To jump on that, I think when it comes to mental-health-related issues, often we'll say, 'Let's direct the child to school counsellor, to an FSC[25] worker or to any other social service practitioner', but in reality, how many of our social service practitioners or school counsellors are well-equipped or trained enough to provide mental health first aid?

Si Qi

What's the difference? As in a counsellor is not equipped to deal with these issues—is it something different for a child?

Cayden

Yeah. So the social service practitioners may have a degree or Masters in counselling, social work or psychology, but they may not have the experience to deal with emotional distress or manage symptoms related to mental health disorders. One may have the formal education or training of a therapy or intervention, but whether he or she is proficient in carrying it out is another matter. This is where continuing education and on-the-job coaching or

[25] FSC: Family Service Centre

supervision are important. I think it's critical that every social service provider or agency should have a certain level of capability or capacity for the staff to be trained in this area.

Even for laymen, I think we also should get trained. We often see campaigns that everyone should go for CPR AED[26] training. Why not mental health training as well? We should make mental health first aid as common as CPR AED. Just like every Grassroots leader, every layman, every auntie and uncle can go to a CC[27] to sign up for a CPR AED course. A mental health first aid course should be that available as well, so that when it comes to, for instance my nephew, my niece or any child that faces emotional distress, I know how to first respond, what I can do as a first responder, and what I can do to render that quick support. Of course, if things become more complicated, then I know where to direct the child to for further support. So we should make this as common as CPR AED.

EVERYONE DESERVES TO FEEL BETTER

Si Qi

Do you guys have any last words or message you would like to leave the readers with about mental health?

Jeremy

I think the first one would be that mental health is as important as physical health. It is more difficult to diagnose, it is more difficult to be seen, but it affects the individual just as physical health would at every level.

---

[26] CPR AED: A course that empowers an individual to perform Cardiopulmonary resuscitation (CPR) and use the Automated External Defibrillator (AED) when called upon.

[27] CC: Community Centre

The second one would be that if we zoom out, mental health is really important because the impact of mental health passes on through generations. We talk about poverty and the intergenerational transmission of poverty—how a lower-income family may pass on the impact of poverty and perpetuate related issues to their future generations. Mental health can have that kind of impact as well. If the child is in a family with multiple adverse childhood experiences—lack of warmth, no stable family, they will have their own mental health concerns and that may be passed on to the next generation.

Cayden

I feel that everyone deserves to feel better. It starts with paying attention to yourself and your needs, because oftentimes we pay so much attention to others and to the tangible things. How to make others happy? Should I get a pay raise? Should I get a car? Should I get a house? But your pursuit of your own mental wellbeing is very important. Everyone deserves to feel better.

CHAPTER 6

Setting Our Youths Up For A Healthy State Of Mind

By Joel Wong, Social Worker, TOUCH Community Services

Joel entered the social work field because of how he was personally impacted by the help he received from his support network when his father passed away from cancer during his teens. Today, he teaches a mental health programme to youths, and stresses the importance of the role parents play in building resilience in their children from young so that they are prepared and equipped to face the ups and downs in life.

LOSING MY DAD TO CANCER

Si Qi

What got you interested in social work and mental health?

Joel

I think for me, what got me into social work was that when I was growing up . . .
[short pause]

. . . I lost my dad to cancer. I was sixteen years old. At that point in time, there were a lot of emotions that I went through. I was feeling really upset and did not know how to deal with the overwhelming emotions by channelling them somewhere. I was really thankful for the support from the professionals, my teachers, my family members, even church members who rallied alongside to support me. And that prevented me, I suppose, from developing any kind of mental health condition at that time. So I think that was when I first understood the importance of support that I'm aware not a lot of people may have.

When I was in university studying social work, two of my friends who also had a similar heart for mental health work roped me in to start a mental health awareness campaign with the support of TOUCH Community Services. Initially, the campaign was called The Make A Difference Race. It was a public awareness run bringing together people together from all walks of life—people with mental health issues, the community, and the mental health professionals—to make a stand and say that mental health issues don't just affect a specific group of people, they can affect anyone, and we need to give a greater voice towards the cause. Subsequently, we rebranded the campaign to Light of Hope. The intent was to focus on the message of hope in the midst of darkness, in the midst of difficult times, which was really the story that a lot of us went through.

After I graduated, I continued my work in the mental health arena by serving the community as a social worker with TOUCH.

HOW DO WE TEACH YOUTHS ABOUT MENTAL HEALTH?

Si Qi

Could you share more about your mental health programme? I think it's the Do You M.I.N.D? programme, right?

Joel

Yes, it's the Do You M.I.N.D? programme. We realized that many students and youths between the age of thirteen and seventeen don't really have a good understanding of the different issues or conditions surrounding mental health. This programme was created to raise mental health awareness among this group of youths. We created an interactive three-hour programme where we educate students about the different mental health conditions, how they can cope, and also confront the big misconception that mental health issues will not affect any of them. Because they're still so young, they think that *aiyah I will never develop that condition.* But oftentimes why they might think that way is because they might not have faced a big issue in their life before, or they might not realize that at some point in their life, they will have to cope with something that's difficult. So we want to try and equip all of them with the right skills to make them more resilient to mental health issues, teach them coping mechanisms which they can embrace, and support them in having a positive mental wellbeing in their lives.

Si Qi

Nice! So the thing is, I think for people who don't know what mental health is or they've not experienced it personally or witnessed it around them right, it is hard for them to know what mental health is. So how do you guys explain to the youths what mental health is, especially for those of them who are like, *huh, what is it?*

Joel

A three-hour programme can seem very long. So we break the curriculum into five different stations and we cover a total of four key mental health issues affecting youths in Singapore—major depressive disorders, generalized anxiety disorders, eating disorders, and self-harm behaviours. Self-harm behaviours are not really a mental health condition, but it's one of the signposts of a possible mental health condition, and that's why we want to focus on that too. In the three hours, we focus very clearly on the key things that we want the youths or students to take away with them and we keep things bite-sized and relevant. For example, by using recent examples of media personalities who have shared their stories and trying to bring these examples down to everyday situations that students might find themselves in. By using some of these examples and making it relevant to them, we hope that they'll be able to see how mental health is a big part of their life.

CAN GOOGLE TELL YOU IF YOU'RE DEPRESSED?

Joel

We also have a segment where students can ask us any questions that they may have. A common question is 'I think I have a mental health condition because I did this test on Google. Is it accurate?'

Si Qi

Ohh!!

Joel

And that's a really big misconception that students have. Just because a Google test of ten questions tells them they have depression, they choose to believe so, and that's really unfortunate. So we try and correct that misunderstanding by telling them that actually the test involved for any mental health condition is a lot more specific and having a diagnosis is much more serious than what Google can tell you. We explain that only a psychiatrist is able to make a diagnosis for mental health conditions.

Si Qi

That's really interesting because I think, obviously youths are growing up in the internet age, and it has grown much bigger than what you and I experienced when we were growing up. So I think it's a double-edged sword, because there is a lot more information out there, but also a lot more misinformation.

Joel

Definitely. I think one of the things that I've noticed from our social media outreach on Instagram and TikTok, is that there are online profiles that encourage self-harm behaviours and are pro-eating disorders in nature, which is extremely dangerous. These groups share their own experiences not in the hopes of overcoming it, but in the hopes of encouraging other people to follow their journey and even join them. I'm not sure about its prevalence in Singapore, but we do see a lot of these profiles online. This is another concern that we have, about how open the internet has been. There are plenty of opportunities for us to correct these misunderstandings. So we go on these platforms, encourage users who express that they are feeling down, and correct the myth about mental health issues. But at the same time, we're also combating these online accounts that encourage behaviours that are dangerous.

Si Qi

That's really thought-provoking.

IT'S A LEVELS OR NOTHING

Si Qi

In your line of work, what are some of the mental health stigmas that you've observed among our youths today?

Joel

I think a lot of youths believe that mental health issues can affect anyone, but they do not believe that it can happen to themselves. Internationally, one in five people will develop a mental health condition at some point in their lives. When I share this figure to the students, in a class of forty students, that's eight students who potentially would develop a mental health condition in their lifetime. So that really hits home to them and breaks that myth that mental health issues cannot affect them.

I think another misunderstanding or stigma that a lot of students face is that they do not want to receive help when they are going through something difficult because of the belief that it's a sign of weakness. So we have had youths who come to us for counselling and initially, they resisted because of the fear that people would look upon them as weak, that they're not resilient enough, or just not good enough.

Another stigma surrounding the recovery from mental health issues is that people tend to believe that it is a long-drawn-out process. A lot of times, the recovery process is longer because the individual might have sought help very late as opposed to earlier on. If help is sought earlier on, sometimes even before the onset of the condition itself, the recovery process can be much shorter. Seeking help early is so important.

Si Qi

Yeah, and so it's interesting that you mentioned that help, if sought earlier on, or even before the onset of the condition, is actually better than later. But the tricky thing is when you are dealing with a lot of academic stress and you look left or right—everyone is dealing with the same thing. It normalizes it and you think *oh, this is just how it is.* So it's very hard to identify and connect with yourself and understand that *hey, am I going through something that is maybe not so healthy?* So how do we get people to understand this a bit better?

Joel

Yep. That's why it's important for us to go down to the schools and educate students about the importance of taking care of their own mental wellbeing. For example, I remember my time in JC[28]. JC is known very much for its stressful two years, because you try and cram so many things in those two years, right? I remember in J1 during lunch time especially, the canteen would be full, but my peers weren't eating in the canteen. They were studying! Their textbooks were open! The stress can really get to you.

Nonetheless, I think it's very important to teach the different signs of mental health issues, and I believe that students today do benefit from having greater access to a lot of this information online. But what they need to learn is how to put into practice some of the de-stressing skills, how to schedule time to relax, and set aside time to talk to people about how they're feeling. I think that can really benefit them if they're able to do that.

Si Qi

As you're talking about your JC, I also remember my own JC time and I think it's quite crazy because in the morning before assembly, everyone would be in the canteen studying. Especially when it was leading up to the A Levels period, it was just quiet.

[28] JC: Junior College

Like pin-drop silence, everyone was just studying. It brings a chill down my spine like, oh my gosh, we were quite . . . It's quite crazy! [Si Qi laughs]

Joel

Even during the bus ride to school, it is so common to see students studying on the bus. I remember even right up to the national anthem or the school song, my schoolmates would have their books on the ground while they're standing up, but they're not singing the anthem, they're just looking down at the textbook. And I always wonder, how much can you cram in the last moment? It's just adding on to the stress.

Si Qi

Right. Maybe we can dive a little bit into this. So I'm one of the people who has A Levels trauma. A Levels was very traumatic for me. One of the things I felt back then was that A levels was this huge race to the end. I remember thinking to myself that once I get past this right, it's like a certain level of achievement is unlocked after you cross this line. And because during the A Levels studying stage, you also plan ahead a lot into university and think about your career. And so I did think a little bit about my life beyond A levels, and I realized that after A Levels, it's actually not the end because I still had to go to university and take exams anyway and get a degree. And I was like okay, so, what's next after my degree? I'll probably go into an office and strive for promotions and KPIs. So at that time, I was a little bit cognizant of the fact that I was already in the rat race. But I didn't have the space to really think about this because I was so preoccupied with studying. I didn't have time to make sense of what I really wanted in life. I just knew I had to score well first, think later.

So I think this is quite telling of a Singaporean culture where we're not given the space to really think about what we want to do

in life or the options we have. And I don't know if you agree with that, but I think that contributes a lot to the stress that youths face because it's very heavy—it's all or nothing. It's either you get your A Levels, or, *shit.*
[laughter]

Joel

Yeah, I guess. I can kind of relate to that a little bit because when I was in J1, I remember failing every single subject. I actually wanted to drop out of JC and go to polytechnic because there was this kind of belief at that point in time that maybe the polytechnic route might be less stressful or easier. I now know that's not true. But at that point in time, I just wanted to give in. However, that's when the family support came in. My mom told me 'It doesn't matter whether at the end of the day you make it or not, but you need to finish it and give it your best and see where it goes from there'. So in that sense, having that support from people who really mattered to me was also very important.

I would count myself rather privileged in that sense because I can imagine and recall many of my classmates who probably didn't have that same level of support. They were always ranting about how they were feeling stressed that they would not match up to their siblings or that they would not be able to do well enough to get into, say, a doctor or a lawyer kind of education track because their older siblings are all doctors or studying to be doctors. Even now, as I think back on my education life, my parents were never the kind who said 'You must always get straight As'. They were more of, 'As long as you're happy, you do your best, then we're happy'. And I think that kind of really enabled me to do what I want and pursue what I want as well without having that at the back of my mind like *I need to do this because they want this*, which I would imagine a lot of students experience.

Si Qi

Yeah, the role of the family and the role of the parents is very important. How do you think we can encourage parents to understand and empathize with their kids' stress a bit more?

Joel

I think, definitely, a lot of advocacy work. I think we have to do a lot of parent engagement work on how they can support their child in the stressful academic world. I remember we were at one of the JCs for a parents' talk, and the parents were asking how they can support their child better. For sure, we can teach your child how to do deep-breathing exercises, journal, and craft out self-care routines. But parents also play a very important role, if not more important than us as professionals. For example, we hear of how some parents say 'I allow my child to play games and relax as long as they show me their results are doing well', but then that's a cause-and-effect thing. You have to do something before I give you something, and that may not always be the best approach to take, especially if they're playing the game to destress, for example. Of course, we need to set boundaries. We're not saying give a blank cheque, but how we communicate, that is also very important. So educating parents, providing them with some of the skill sets—that's also very important.

RESILIENCE EDUCATION STARTS YOUNG

Si Qi

Yeah, and on this topic . . . Let's say you flunk your A Levels or O Levels or whatever really badly, and it's quite *jialat*[29]. Maybe you have to fork out a lot of money to go to a private university or you have to go out to work first, or something. I think people can feel really lousy after that happens, or feel really ashamed and guilty.

---

[29] Jialat: Singapore slang that describes a dire situation

How do we pick ourselves up from those kinds of situations? From failure, especially.

Joel

Yeah, I mean this topic on failure is really interesting. My own view is that a child needs to learn how to cope with failure, even from a young age. That includes being able to deal with disappointments. For example, if a child wants to play on the iPad, and the parents say no because of various reasons, it is common for the child to cry or throw a tantrum. That's a normal reaction, but it is also an opportunity for the child to learn how to cope with the disappointment because in life there will be many disappointments! Yet in those situations, it is so common for parents to simply give the iPad to stop the tantrums.
[laughter]

Joel

If the first major disappointment that a child faces is at the A Levels, I think we have to reflect on the reasons why the child was not exposed to dealing with disappointments earlier. I think most children today grow up in very sheltered environments where they're sheltered from failure. Parents try and give them the best and ensure that everything they do is a success. It's not the fault of the parents in the sense that we all want the best for our child. But at the same time, 'I think some of these opportunities for the child to learn needs to include the processing of disappointments'.

Si Qi

And what are some of these tools to deal with setbacks?

Joel

For example, if a child acts out from being disappointed that he's not able to play games or watch a certain movie at a particular time, it's important for the parents to not give in, and to process with the child after that. It's not just about allowing the child to cry it out and that's it, peace when they stop. Bring it to the next step—spend that time to talk to the child and process their feelings. *Earlier on when you were crying, why were you upset? Why were you disappointed?* And explore those feelings, explore the reasons behind them. Maybe a child would say 'I was upset because I really wanted to play the game and then you said no'. After that, ask and teach the child, 'Is crying always the right way, or is that the only way? What other ways are there to try and overcome it? And while you're crying, were there other things that maybe you could have done?'

Another thing would be the involvement of the parents. How involved are the parents in the child's growing up years? In a lot of cases that we see today, the child is left to their own devices, literally mobile devices. And parents are saying *I need to work* and all, and they're not spending enough time to really just have good conversations with their child. And I'm not saying just sitting there and being present physically, but also being able to emotionally connect with the child. With my clients, when they share something important with me, I ask if they have shared it with their parents. And they're like *no, why would I want to share it with them?* And I find that so sad. I would be devastated if my children are not able to share all these things with me. I think it's so important that they're able to share and open up about what they're feeling. I want them to be able to trust me with their emotions. It takes hard work, definitely.

Si Qi

Nice! If you had a message you would like to share with the readers of the book about mental health, what would that be?

Joel

Positive mental wellbeing is important for everyone, and if you're going through a difficult time, talk to somebody about it. You're not alone, and there are many people out there who want to support you.

Si Qi

Thank you very much.

CHAPTER 7

Cultivating Integrity Between What We're Learning And What We're Experiencing

By Narasimman S/O Tivasiha Mani, Director, Volunteer Development, Co-head of Mental Health Care, Impart Ltd

Mental health education needs to go beyond the classrooms. Through working with youths, Narash highlights that youths need to see how the theories they learn in the classroom can be applied in their own lives. He hopes that mental health education can become more immersive and integrated with everyday experiences.

WE HAVE TO COME TO GRIPS WITH OUR OWN MENTAL HEALTH

MK

What inspired you to start Impart?

Narash

Impart was started quite some time ago together with some young people to explore how the community can enable reintegration for youths who were formerly placed in juvenile rehabilitation institutes. Many of them are not reintegrated into society, and one tangible marker is that they struggle to complete their national examinations. As I focused on supporting the reintegration efforts, I realized that many of them were struggling to study for their N Levels. However, there weren't any volunteers able and willing to connect with these high-risk youths in community spaces. This seemed to be a gap in the ecosystem where only professionals were involved. So Impart started out by providing academic tutoring, where ordinary volunteers supported these youths through their examinations.

But as I did this reintegrative work, mental health became a large part of necessary intervention. Many of the youths we were supporting came from marginalized communities and were experiencing a lot of psychological adversities and mental health challenges which were constantly neglected or undetected—one of the key reasons why education wasn't a top priority for them. This neglect was perpetuated by the kind of volunteerism trends back then, where volunteers typically focused on helping people with 'bread and butter issues' rather than things of the mind. Eventually, we responded by piloting a project where volunteers are trained and equipped with coping skills to help youths out there facing psychological adversities.

MK

Got it. What are some mental health stigmas you see when you work with youths on the ground?

Narash

I work with a wide range of young people. For a lot of them, achievements and success are of priority. So if you tell a university student that *hey, you may need a mental health break*, they may not understand what you're talking about. For them, *as long as I'm successful, that means my mental health is good.* They may even equate success with mental wellness. However, I know that mental health plays an integral role in our emotional, psychological, and social wellbeing, and so it has to be the priority.

I work with young people, typically university students or young adults, to help them in their journey of giving back to other young people. In their process of giving back, what sometimes happens is that they have to come to grips with their own mental health or their childhood trauma. Giving and helping other people may not be something that we typically do, and it may not even be something that we're comfortable with, but sometimes it also makes us face our own realities or struggles. When that happens, I may have to suggest for them to see a therapist. It's very interesting—I am doing mental health work together with them, they're all taught about mental health skills, but even in the midst of all that, people say to me *I don't need therapy*. Some people say *I'm not like the youth that I serve*. But the truth of the matter is mental health is not a respecter of persons. Everyone can go for therapy, even myself. And one does not need to wait until extreme mental health symptoms show up to seek therapy.

MK

Exactly.

Narash

When a lot of people only seek to treat it when they experience extreme symptoms, then the stigma of mental health deepens or the incidences of mental illnesses increase. The idea that you need to have something really serious happening with you before you go and see a mental health professional is dangerous. And I think that's the most challenging stigma.

MK

Got it. What do you think is stopping people from seeking help?

Narash

What is stopping people? I think number one is what we just spoke about—the stigma. Some of these stigmas seem to have their roots in how Asian cultures perceive mental health. There seems to be a deep shame when we experience mental illness symptoms. A lot of people grapple with mental health as I am not good enough if I have a mental health issue. They do not treat it like a headache, cough, or flu where they might just be unwell for a while, perhaps get some treatment, before returning to normalcy again. For them it becomes like 丢脸[30], as some Chinese people say, throw face.[31] Some Malay people may also say to me that it's very malu[32], or it's because the individual is not spiritually strong enough hence they are possessed by evil spirits. Indian people may see it as karma or possession by evil spirits, and may not even want to touch the topic—it's a big taboo as some people feel that a person with mental health issues will diminish the honour and reputation of the whole family.

When we associate mental health with our identity, or when our culture ties mental health to self-worth, it increases the

---

[30] 丢脸: Mandarin phrase meaning embarrassment or loss of dignity

[31] Throw face: Direct translation of 丢脸

[32] Malu: Malay phrase meaning embarrassment

shame and deeply influences our silence surrounding mental health challenges. Because it's like saying *yeah, you're not good and you're an embarrassment.* And if people know that you have a mental health record, they may see you differently, and in a society like Singapore that often focuses on economic achievements, employers might even disqualify you during the hiring process as they might have the impression that having a mental health issue will impede your capabilities and productivity. If these misconceptions about mental health are not dispelled, it will continue to instill fear and deter people from seeking help early.

'Another common reason stopping people from seeking help is that they do not know that they're not doing well due to poor mental health literacy or a lack of awareness about the need for treatment. Perhaps they are displaying signs of burnout, but they might think it's just stress, that I'm okay, I just need a little break'. But some of these things are not as simple as taking a break or a vacation. 'If mental health symptoms can be resolved by taking a break or doing a self-care activity, I would say that they are more lifestyle-related issues'. That being said, regardless of the severity of your symptoms, initiating, engaging, and participating in your own mental health work can make a world of a difference. If you still feel unwell after taking a break, self-care, or other self-regulating activities, you may need to see a therapist as part of the treatment process because you're having more debilitating symptoms, and there's nothing wrong with that! There is no one-size-fits-all model for treatment, and we need to educate people about the treatment options available. Unfortunately, denial, avoidance, or unawareness will only delay the eventual need for mental health treatment.

Finally, a poor perception of what the mental health professionals are or the level of trust in the field of mental health services may also stop people from seeking help. Maybe they've had a poor experience with a counsellor before. Or they've heard about what visiting a psychiatrist is like from their friend's experience, and they form a perception of how the mental health service is going to be, which creates a barrier especially if their friend's experience was not great. People start to think *oh, they're just trying to medicate me, they're not trying to listen to me, I don't want to take medication as I'm scared of the side effects.* And until they understand that mental health treatments don't always have to be that way, they may never seek treatment.

BUILDING A COORDINATED MENTAL HEALTH ECOSYSTEM

MK

Listening to your sharing, it seems like intervention needs to take place at different levels, whether it is from an individual or a community level. How can communities facilitate the removal of stigmas, or encourage people to look for support or help? Because I think this is relevant to what you're trying to do with Impart as well.

Narash

So firstly, I think that we do not have a robust network of care when it comes to mental health in the community. Many organizations seem to be working in silos when it comes to mental health. I often hear people tell me that 'Oh if you have this issue then you need to go to IMH[33]', instead of turning to immediate community resources where one can seek help. I think this deepens the problem for us.

Basically, we do not have sufficient primary levels of care. Primary levels of care can be things like imparting coping, regulation, or interpersonal skills and empowering people to utilize these skills in times of distress. Something that Impart

[33] IMH: Institute of Mental Health (Singapore's only hospital dedicated to mental health)

is trying to do now is to teach coping skills to young people. And when we talk about coping skills, it's not just one or two types of skills. There are a lot of coping skills that people can learn, and the coping skills that fits me may not fit you. How you cope and how I cope may be very different. So the youths in the programme that we run have to go through a whole set of skills before they identify what works and doesn't work for them. This means that there is a lot of trial and error through learning and actually implementing it in their own lives. When people have a set of coping skills, it can help them through times of distress, and this means that we're not going to flood the tertiary levels, like in IMH. Furthermore, skills-building through primary levels of care can prepare people for therapy. These skills can help in preparing the individual to talk to a mental health professional, and can also help in stabilizing the individual which can speed up the therapy process too. I feel that it is important for Singapore to focus on primary levels of care right now.

At the secondary levels of care, people talk and journey with others in the community or through counselling, and maybe some levels of psychotherapy without pharmacotherapy—medication. And the tertiary levels is where it involves pharmacotherapy together with the psychiatrist, psychologist and the community working together. I think there are semblances of it in our society, but we can do better in terms of coordinated support and work on this front, and it starts with building a strong foundation of primary care. Does that answer the question?

MK

It does, it does. I'm actually thinking . . . I think one of the components necessary for people to look for help is also a safe space. People want to be heard and to feel that they're being understood. So I'm just wondering, how can we collectively do this better? How can we be more present in life? How can we actively listen better? How can we co-create safe spaces for one another to live in so that we're more open to talk about difficult emotions and issues?

Narash

I really like the word you just used—co-creating spaces. I think first, it takes organizations to come together to see how we can co-create these spaces. I think this question can only be answered when organizations band together to see how we do even the first cut of things—referrals. How do I refer my client to you without the client having to repeat everything from this organization to the next? How do we create a referral system that doesn't send clients scrambling around different organizations, but rather, creates a safe space which says, *hey, we understand the issue you're facing, let's try to see how we can coordinate our services to help you.* I believe that when organizations work together, we can be fully focused on the person's experience and can find ways to make mental health treatment more accessible.

Another way to create safe spaces is to consider unconventional treatment protocols—

MK

Tell me more.

Narash

A lot of people in the community, based on the way we have structured mental healthcare, think that they have to come to institutions to see a professional who will provide the services. But what WHO[34] is telling us is that many people are not seeking help, or that they are seeking help a lot later than they should. So shouldn't there be some sort of outreach model to go out there

[34] WHO: World Health Organization

and help people? Yes, a lot of work is done around stigmatization. There are a lot of Instagram posts and campaigns coming around stigmatization, and there are a lot of conversations around mental health that have risen after COVID. It has increased exponentially. But I think stigma in the community doesn't go away by just talking about it. There needs to be deeper involvement of the community to address the stigma.

MK

Yeah.

Narash

What we need are liberating experiences that shed stigma. So the question for us as a community is, *how can we create a non-conventional way of doing treatment in the community such that it reduces stigma and makes things normal?* Like *eh, this is normal, we all can talk about how we cope with our mental health.* You and I can talk about it without feeling scared or vulnerable. So finding non-conventional treatment or outreach models outside of the treatment room setting, I think, would be an important hurdle to overcome in order to bring this conversation to the next level. It's not just about talking about it. It's not just about having more campaigns. It's about bringing the message to the people through their experiences in whatever environment they may be in—be it at school, work, or in religious settings, etcetera.

For example, I would like to turn our attention to university students. I think we have heard about some university students committing suicide. We've heard about university students who are victims of hazing, bullying or sexual harassment. And I think destigmatization and helping them receive treatment is not just about creating a space where they can go and receive counselling. It's about integrating some kind of mental health curriculum into their everyday spaces. It's about having some kind of coach or mentor that goes in and says *hey, can I check in with you* or *let's talk about what are you grappling with?* And going on to share practical coping skills or mental health strategies they can employ. Such experiences can change how they perceive or experience mental healthcare and how they experience the destigmatization of mental health in the way they interact with people or professionals. I believe that is a lot more valuable than just talking about it. I'm not saying that talking about it is not good, I think having these conversations and all that are great, but it's not impactful enough.

INCORPORATING MENTAL HEALTH CURRICULUMS THAT ARE FELT AND EXPERIENCED

MK

Anything you want to share with me about your work and the trends you have been observing on the ground?

Narash

I think that as of late, there have been a lot of young people, really young people, experiencing mental health symptoms. And when we talk about young people, I'm referring to primary school students—I've been talking to primary schools—where there seem to be children who are experiencing mental health symptoms. I think this is a worrying trend that tells us we need to have some kind of mental health curriculum. Not just a curriculum that cognitively feeds the mind, but a mental health curriculum that is felt and experienced by the children and youths. We don't want the mental health curriculum to be like a theoretical lesson on swimming in classrooms without the practical experience of being in a pool and learning how to swim. It can't be in such a way where I can be talking about the techniques of swimming, but there isn't an experience of it in the pool, and worse still, we need to venture out into the open sea.

For example, when someone is unable to regulate themselves, we can teach them regulation strategies and coping mechanisms, but schools need more than that in their mental health curriculums. It is like expecting a person to drive a car after theory lessons without having a practical session or an instructor beside you. The schools need embedded mental health strategies and systems to manage some of these situations where the youths are dysregulated or in distress. We need to allow the youths to experience it so that there's some level of integrity and congruence between what they're learning about mental health and what they're experiencing in school and how the adults around them view mental health.

How youths view mental health will be enhanced through experiential learning. It can be experienced through hearing how their teachers talk about it. It can be experienced from seeing how the teacher manages their own stress. I think it's okay to tell the youths that 'I'm managing something right now'. It helps them and makes you feel human. So sometimes even with my own clients or youths I serve, if they share with me something that I feel is quite stressful, I'll say 'Wow, that sounds stressful to me as well, when they share that. Why not, we take a breather right now? That sounds very stressful, let's breathe together'. Or let's drink a cup of cold water to just let that topic simmer down a little bit, then we go back and talk about it again. But what I'm modelling to them is also how I'm coping. Hence, teachers modelling how they care for their own mental health normalizes the fact that everyone needs time to cope with our emotions. This helps to gain acceptance that mental health is part of our life experience. If not, there might be a disconnect and a profound lack of empathy and identification. This will pave way for dehumanizing treatment towards youths in distress where they can be sent to the counselling room and it can feel like they are being sent to the detention room. It can bring a lot of humiliation, shame, and negativity. So I think that's important how young people experience systems surrounding mental healthcare in their school.

CHAPTER 8

Conscious Parenting: Raising Yourself First

By Jenny Ng, Conscious Parenting Coach

The conscious parenting movement is one that advocates for parents to reflect on the reasons their child behaves in a certain way and find out what their internal needs are. Jenny shares how conscious parenting actually helps parents to operate from a place of love rather than a place of fear, and how it helps children develop emotional literacy from young.

THE GIFT OF UNCONDITIONAL LOVE

Jenny

So at thirty-five years old, my biological clock was ticking away, and I was curious about becoming a mother. What would I be like as a mum? Would I be the same, or would I be different?

In my motherhood journey, my child has taught me lots of things. One night while I was breastfeeding her, her index finger touched my face, and it felt like a magical touch. I felt like *wow*, all this while, I thought we parents were the ones who gave children unconditional love, but at that moment, I realized that she was also giving me unconditional love—no matter who I was in the past, present or future. I was so moved because most parents are like, *you have to achieve this, you have to be good, you have to get good grades, learn the piano.* When my child gave me this magical touch, and accepted me for who I was and who I was not, it completely changed my understanding of unconditional love. So I switched over to pursue family education. I took up a master's program, and from there I transitioned from web development to family education. That was in 2012.

At the same time, I started Nannies on Wheels, a social enterprise training people forty and above with empty nest syndrome, single parents, retirees, relief childcare educarers, to go to parents' houses to take care of children. It's not just about taking care and making sure they are safe, but it's also about bringing purposeful, age-appropriate activities to the children. But we are looking at closing it down to allow me to focus on conscious parenting work full-time. I used to work at the parenting department of an early childhood education training institute. I have followed Dr Shefali since 2016, who founded the conscious parenting movement, and when she said *parents need to first raise themselves before they raise their kids,* I was like *ohhhhh, this is what I want.*

[Jenny laughs]

HEALING THE INNER CHILD

MK

I see. What are some of the stigmas that you've observed as you work with parents on the ground?

Jenny

In Singapore, I find that parents are not quite open-minded. It's not right or wrong—it's more about the society we live in. When I run parenting workshops in Singapore, I see more questions around *how can I fix my child?* How to get them quiet, get them focused, get them to sit down and do homework. A lot of parenting models are about that—like common sense parenting, which is about how you can talk to your child so that they can listen to you.

Conscious parenting is more about, *okay, how can I first connect with my child at her level? If she isn't doing homework right now, what is behind this behaviour?* Not doing homework is only the behaviour that is exhibited—what could be her internal needs? It could be *oh, I don't know how to do it and I am frustrated.* Or it could be *oh, earlier on in school, something happened and I'm not in the mood to do homework.* It's about getting parents to support their children at that level. At times, if the child is not ready to tell you, just sit there and accompany her until she's ready. In Singapore's context, we are more focused on the *doing*. So the *being* is very uncomfortable.

MK

The being—yes! The *being*.

Jenny

Yes, the being. It's very uncomfortable for the parents.

MK

That was what I was thinking of in my head right before you said that. The freedom to be.

Jenny

Yes, freedom to be. You are asking parents to sit down there and not do anything. That's not in their comfort zone. They'll be thinking *I must do something! I must do something to prove that I'm a good parent, or a good adult.*

MK

And we don't realize that we're actually trapping our own kids. We're actually putting them in a prison, and the kids become prisoners in the prison. You know the irony? In a prison, there must be a guard, but the guard is also in the prison. So what kind of relationship is that, really, if there is a lack of freedom to be?

Jenny

Yeah, it's quite toxic. Both parent and child don't have the freedom to be who they are, to explore who they are freely because they don't have time to explore, really.

MK

I don't have time, I don't have space, I've got work. We're so caught up by the busyness of life that sometimes we don't recognize or remember what is important. And oftentimes, as a compensation model, we can't even sit still by ourselves, with ourselves, because there's so much out there that we're trying to run away from. So we tend to look for other people as a compensation for that, and that doesn't really solve the equation, does it?

Jenny

It doesn't. In the end, parents still need to heal their inner child inside. One of the things I learned about myself is that honesty is very important to me. So last year, during home-based learning, when I discovered that my child was playing games when she should be doing homework without telling me, I would get triggered. I would sit down and ask 'Why are you not telling mummy that you are playing games? It's okay if you tell me, then we can reserve that time to play games'. I could feel that I was very stern, and not freeing up, and like *ugh*, *control control control*! And she's like, 'I don't want to tell you because you will say ALL this' . . . And this was what she wanted to avoid. When I realized that, I said 'Okay, sorry, mummy is not comfortable with you not telling me'. So I changed my tonality, because I realized that when I paused, I could switch around to say that that was not the energy I wanted to give my child. I calmed down.

After that, I found out why honesty is important to me—but this one needed a bit of work lah because it's to track back what happened during childhood. When I was 11 years old, I was about to go for a dance performance, but I couldn't find one of the accessories that was part of the costume. And just nice on the bench, there was a pair of the accessories that I needed, so I took it and put it on. Then later, one of my peers couldn't find her accessories.

MK

Oh no!

Jenny

Yeah, I know, right? I was like, *I cannot tell, I cannot tell, because I need that and I cannot find mine.* So I couldn't tell the truth, and my teacher was rushing to help her fix the costume. So, that incident really hit me. So, why honesty was so important to me was because at that point in time I interpreted the incident as *I cannot trust myself because I wasn't honest.*

MK

Therefore, you expect other people to be honest as a compensation.

Jenny

Yes, that's right. So I want my child to be honest as well. So it's like the emotion you have about whatever behaviour your child is exhibiting reflects what's inside you. And then if you can realize that, go and heal that. Sometimes it could be the inner child we're talking about because of unmet needs, or sometimes it could be the external things that triggered an emotion.

OPERATING FROM A PLACE OF LOVE AND NOT FEAR

Si Qi

It's really cool because yesterday, I interviewed another psychologist and she was also sharing that a lot of mental health issues basically have roots in our childhood, and that's her experience—that it rarely comes out of nowhere. It really always has roots in our childhood, and as adults, we need to reparent ourselves.

Jenny

Yes!

Si Qi

And I want to hear from you, because I think that there is some disconnect between mental health and all these other parenting things. It's not so clear why parenting relates to mental health, why certain parenting styles might cause my child to have anxiety, or develop certain negative traits in the future. Are you able to draw that link for us?

Jenny

Okay, so just now what MK said about needing compensation or recognition from parents—I had that too when I was young. I thought I didn't deserve love because my parents expected me, as the eldest, to grow up fast. When you're growing up that way, even when you're a young adult making money already, when your parents question your ability to make good decisions, for instance, your career advancement, you go into the *I'm not good enough* state again. So when parents feel that they aren't enough but aren't healing it, they go into their parenting wanting their child to fulfill that not enough-ness inside.

MK

I was sharing with Jenny about how I started doing transformational work when I was eighteen and I realized that the material world didn't have the answers that I was looking for. No matter how much money, how many results, achievements, or successes I had, it didn't fill up that hole inside me. When I did transformational work, one of the things I came to realize was I spent my whole life chasing after those three marks that I did not get when I was seven for my English paper. And as a result of that, that three per cent started manifesting in all sorts of ways in my life, and I realized that my relentless chase was nothing more but a compensation for that. So that was when Jenny responded by saying that a lot of parents also do it—that we chase after all these little things to fill up something, or impose our own expectations of what we didn't have onto our kids.

Jenny

And to add on to that—it's about whether we are operating from love or operating from fear. So when parents are going *my child needs to be always perfect, get 100 marks,* in order to compensate for the three marks they did not get . . . That is operating from fear because *I wasn't enough, so when I parent my child, I want my child to be better.* I used to have that fear too. This *oh, practice more, you can do better, you can do better.* But my child told me in my face 'I've already done my best, how else do you want me to do it?' So if children are able to say that, then we become aware that *okay this is not about her, it's about me*, and I can reflect on it. But if you say 'How can you talk back to me? You are so disrespectful!' Then, that is running from resistance and fear, and needing your child to fill up your lack. But if you are able to see that and slowly heal your inner child, then you can operate from whole. *I'm whole, I'm complete, I'm not asking for external things to prove that I'm worthy. I'm not asking for my father's affirmation, and I'm not asking my boss for whatever praise I was looking for,* than taking praise as a bonus. When I operate from whole and enough-ness, I can give my child the space to grow into who she or he is. Yeah, so, that is the difference when you're operating from fear or love.

SURRENDER TO WHO YOU ARE

Si Qi

Everyone needs to understand themselves better to have a better life, a more fulfilled life, and to care for the people around us. So, what would you say can encourage people to start this journey of looking into yourself?

Jenny

It takes letting go of *being right.* If I were to reflect back on my own journey and some of my observations of others, it's that you need to be curious about yourself and have the courage to step outside of your comfort zone. I always feel that there's another person in me deep down, and I don't like the outside day-to-day operating me. So who is that deep down inside me? During this journey, I feared that *what if I discover that who I am inside is not someone I want to be?*

Si Qi

Yes, I totally get that.

Jenny

So while you're curious about the possibility of your true self, at the same time, you're like—'Okay, do I really want to go there?' But only when you really open up, accept who you are, and who you are not, will you then have the space to honour your truth and your sovereignty. Only then you can enjoy the liberation and freedom to be. It takes courage to do so.

Si Qi

And I think the scary thing also is that there's a disconnect between our external selves and our internal selves, because we spend all our time trying to meet external expectations and we never even try to live the life that we want to lead. So most people will find that the contrast is huge, and as you get further and further disconnected from yourself, you start to not know who you are inside. And there will be parts of you that you don't like, and I think a lot of people find it difficult to reconcile with that. They can't forgive themselves for the things they don't like.

Jenny

And that part is always about letting go—the release and surrender to resistance because there could be certain things that you keep resisting. It's about surrendering to whatever comes, whether it is good or bad.

Si Qi

I think it's really quite sad because there's so much pain and trauma within families passed down through generations. Your mother was once a child. Your parents were once children too, and they also had their own issues as they were growing up. Your grandparents were also once children and they have their own issues as much as we do and it's sad, that we are not really emphasising on this enough, so that we can have a better world.

Jenny

And also, I think we need to acknowledge the parents who didn't know what to do because they have done their best. They thought that was the best way to raise their children, so they did that. Now, we have the awareness and the tools and the perspectives. So if we really want to go into stigma in the Singapore context . . . I think openness is one. For instance, my husband has a certain way of looking at things because that was how he has been brought up all his life. So once, I invited him to a conscious parenting workshop, which was outside of his comfort zone. And he's all *ugh, I don't want,* and he always chooses to go back to his comfort zone, to feel protected, to be with the things he's familiar with.

Si Qi

But we have blind spots, you see. So we may think we are doing very well in life, we may think everything's going very well—

Jenny

It's that control of *I know my life and I want to run it very smoothly in my own way*. But when you step out, you see a different possibility. It's another kind of excitement in life! That's how we get to energise ourselves and be alive again, because you see the world with a different perspective.

COURAGE TO TAKE THE FIRST STEP

Si Qi

Nice. So if there's one last message you would want to send to the readers of this book about mental health, what would that be?

Jenny

It's okay not to be okay. There's nothing wrong with looking at the part that you're lacking. And just be curious about what you can do about it. And still, at the same time, see what you have done so far, and celebrate your achievements. So in terms of mental health, accept yourself and have that compassion towards yourself. Be able to acknowledge that there are things that you're not doing well at the moment, but you don't have to be afraid. Just take things one step at a time and look at how you can proceed further in your life.
[silence]

Don't know where to start? Just self-check. Stay with yourself. It may not be through meditation, but take fifteen minutes a day to hang out with yourself. If you feel uneasy, check-in with yourself. Hold the space for yourself when you don't know what it is inside you that creates the uneasiness. Perhaps list down what would be the things that give you inner strength in the past and fill yourself up with that. And don't be afraid to seek help.

CHAPTER 9

Supporting Children in Their Mental Health Journeys

By Goh Li Shan, Psychologist, REACH (West), Department of Psychological Medicine, National University Hospital

Li Shan works with young children and youths through an initiative that brings mental health services into the community. Through her work, she found that despite their age, children often face the same struggles as adults. They feel embarrassed about having to see a psychologist, and they understand the stigma that implies that the need to see a doctor only arises because something is innately wrong with them. In order to help children thrive as they grow up, parents and teachers need to talk to their children in an open and supportive way that does not reinforce any stereotype.

IT STARTED WITH A DESIRE TO HELP IMPROVE THE LIVES OF CHILDREN

MK

Can you tell me more about what made you decide to embark on this career path?

Li Shan

I like children, so I had planned to take up a diploma in early childhood. This was back in secondary school, but after thinking about it and talking to my dad, I realized that I was interested in issues that affect not just children, but people across the entire developmental lifespan. As I grew older, I became interested not only in childhood development, but also how people think, why people think the way they do, and that very naturally led me to pursue psychology.

I was about eighteen years old when I came to the decision that I would like to major in psychology in university. I did my undergrad at James Cook University, and the course was very enlightening and interesting. I really enjoyed my undergrad days learning about the different kinds of human behaviour and perception, and the different fields of psychology. So when I graduated, it seemed natural for me to pursue a career in this area. And to be very honest, I'm not good at anything else other than understanding human behaviour and why people do what they do.

I started with a desire to help improve the lives of children who were challenged or suffering in some way. Soon after I graduated from university, I found a job at the Singapore Children's Society. I held one main portfolio during my years there. It was a befriending line known as the Tinkle Friend helpline, which provides support and is basically a listening ear to any child who calls up, who is distressed, who is upset, who is bothered by something, or who just wants to talk about their day. Through doing that, I realized that I really enjoy listening to them, helping them solve problems, and helping them alleviate their distress. So even if I couldn't do much in that capacity, at least I could lend them a listening ear. I felt that it was very meaningful work and I really got to hear about the things that bothered them on a very real, down-to-earth and day-to-day basis. And I also realized that I really liked to hear about their troubles, and I also liked working with others who shared a similar mindset. So it was through my work with Children's Society that I got exposed not just to this programme, Tinkle Friend, but also to working with young people and children in different capacities. I had the chance to run workshops and children's camps. It was basically a very youthful and vibrant environment, and I really got to interact with kids, young people, and hear their thoughts and their voices from the ground.

MK

Great! What is your job now?

Li Shan

Now, I'm working with children and young people in a mental health setting as a psychologist.

MK

Which agency are you with right now?

Li Shan

REACH. We run a community programme initiated by the Ministry of Health back in 2008. The objective of REACH is to bring mental health services into the community so that children and young people who have severe mental health issues don't have to go all the way to the hospital or clinic or IMH[35] to seek treatment. Instead, we bring the service to them. The organization has set up four different regional branches: REACH North, South, East and West. And each branch serves the schools in that region. My team serves schools in the west.

MK

Alright, got it. I understand now.

Li Shan

Yeah. So we work very closely with schools, and that's why a lot of referrals come in through the school system. Parents are not able to make appointments with us directly, so they need to either have the school refer them to us, or go through the polyclinic referral process to refer their child to mental health services.

REACH itself is a national organization which serves children from Primary 1 onwards all the way to Junior College Two, including students in the three-year A level programme.

MK

Are there any challenges that you face in your job?

Li Shan

There are some limits to what we can do because of the way the organization is structured. We conduct brief therapy, and ideally, all our therapy sessions fall within eight sessions. If we need to, we extend the sessions, but we can't provide longer-term therapy. We have a maximum of maybe around twenty sessions. If they need longer-term support, we refer them out. That's how we are able to keep our capacity running to take on new cases. So this

[35] IMH: Institute of Mental Health (Singapore's only hospital dedicated to mental health)

is not for long-term care. And because of the short-term nature of our therapy setup, there are some modalities that work better. For example, some approaches like CBT[36] or other kinds of talk therapy, ACT[37], DBT[38], work better for our population. But I know that children being children, young people being young people, sometimes they don't do very well with talk therapy and might prefer a more expressive form like art therapy or play therapy. These mediums of therapy usually require a longer-term approach. This is something that we're not able to offer them because of the nature and setup of the organization's processes. So what we are able to do instead is to adopt play methods into our therapy structure, in a way that will accommodate the short-term structure of our set up.

MK

They play!

Li Shan

Yes, it's their language. So I guess that's one challenge, but we do what we can. For example, even though I can't conduct a full play therapy session, we do engage them using play methods. I can't call it play therapy because most of us are not trained or certified in that area, but I'll engage them using whatever methods I can to build rapport. That could involve playing with toys with them, playing games with them, even playing music during the session to engage them further. But in terms of the creative approaches, at this point in time, we do not have the means to do actual play or art therapy.

---

[36] CBT: Cognitive Behavioral Therapy

[37] ACT: Acceptance and Commitment Therapy

[38] DBT: Dialectical Behavior Therapy

There's another challenge that I face. The therapy session is with the child or young person, but oftentimes their issues may stem from issues happening in the family. If the parents are arguing, if there's a divorce, if there's conflict going on in the family, it will affect their wellbeing. But over at REACH, at this point in time, we don't offer therapy with the family for every child. We don't have the capacity to offer that for every case we see. We often have to refer them to a family service centre for support with family issues.

IF I GO TO A HOSPITAL, DOES THAT MEAN I'M SICK?

MK

Since you've been on the ground working with children, what are some of the stigmas you see as a pattern when it comes to the mental health of children?

Li Shan

Stigmas. Well, I would say that . . .
[silence]

Li Shan

I don't think it's any different from the stigma that adults may face.

MK

Tell me more.

Li Shan

So even though they are children, some of them do feel embarrassed about having to see a psychologist. But I think that today, stigma is being managed because there are school counsellors now in every school. So the kids are more familiar with the idea, and I think schools do try to push out the message that *it doesn't mean you're crazy or mentally ill, you just need someone to talk to.* But still we do have children who are more sensitive—could be the older ones or teenagers who are concerned. They don't want their schoolmates to know that they need this arrangement with this external person who's coming down to the school to talk to them. They do feel the stigma. And I have parents who resist our recommendations for their child to see a psychiatrist to get medication to help them manage their condition better. The parents tell me that their child asks questions like 'If I go and see the doctor and I have to take medication, does it mean that I'm sick?' So the kids understand this stigma very well. Even though some of them may be very young.

Usually, we advise parents to talk to the child in a very open and supportive way, to refrain from reinforcing the idea that there's something wrong with them because they have to see the psychiatrist or doctor. We advise parents to help the child view it from a different perspective. For example, 'You have some difficulties and challenges, and seeing a doctor will help you to learn some new ways to help you cope with the issue, and seeing the doctor is like an additional measure because the doctor can refer you to another therapist in the hospital who can teach you some skills'. So we do our best to tell parents that they should communicate to the child in a way that doesn't reinforce that negative stigma.

Some teenagers are also very worried that the hospital will leave an official record that they're seeing this doctor. They're worried that it will affect their employment opportunities in the future. 'Should I declare that previously I had a mental illness?' So usually, my advice to them is 'Right now you're fifteen years old and you're receiving therapy and support, which is very good. So we hope that by the time you graduate and you finish your training and come out to work, this will be something that has happened many years ago in the past. And hopefully by that time, you are coping well, you are healthy, and doing well in life'. And at that point in time if they're no longer affected emotionally or mentally, then I think it's really up to the candidate's discretion whether or not they wish to disclose this to the potential employer. Because this would have been something that the young adults experienced back in their teenage years, and if by that point in time they're coping well in life, then there's no reason for them to bring it up when they're looking for a job in the future.

So the kids are aware of these stigmas. That's why I say I don't think that it's any different from the stigmas that the adults face with regards to their mental health issues.

THE OPPORTUNITY TO TOUCH THEIR LIVES

MK

What is something that really moved you when working with these kids? I mean, it takes a lot of energy to do this work. What makes it worthwhile to keep on persisting and continuing on in this journey?

Li Shan

I think it's an opportunity to touch their lives. Although it's not the easiest of jobs, I do think that I'm very privileged to have this opportunity to come into the life of a young person who is struggling emotionally or mentally, with family issues, whatever stresses, and make some changes and teach them some new skills. Hopefully, I can change their perspective, help them change the way they think, the way they look at things, and help them to cope. However small the impact I make, I hope I will be able to help them overcome this challenge so that many years later when they look back on their lives, they will think *oh, when I was growing up, I had this issue, but I had good teachers that supported me. I had a good school counsellor and I had this therapist who came every week to talk to me and taught me something.* Even if they can't remember my name, it's okay. But it would be good to know that I entered their life for a reason and managed to help them at that point in time.

MK

What's the driving force behind that? Was there something that inspired you to do this?

Li Shan

Well, for me, I've been very lucky, very blessed. I grew up with very supportive caregivers. And during my time in primary and secondary school, there was no such thing as school counsellors, so if I had a problem, I was basically left to figure it out myself. This was the same for all those who grew up in my era. But I'm very lucky that I had encouraging and supportive adults who took very good care of me. So now that I'm an adult, I would like to have that same opportunity to give back to the younger ones. Of course, I'm not their relative or caregiver, but I would like to have this opportunity to support them. And I do think that it's good for them to have resources like school counsellors and psychologists who they can talk to—something that I never had when I was growing up. So I'm glad that I can play that role now, at least to some of the children and youth whom I see.

DON'T BE AFRAID OF CHALLENGES, BUT DON'T BE AFRAID TO SEEK HELP WHEN YOU NEED IT

MK

What are some of the transformations that you hope to see in the mental health space in Singapore so that these children can be further impacted?

Li Shan

Well, I would hope that stigma can gradually be reduced so that children feel free to express their concerns and voice out their struggles. If they are facing challenges, they can readily find resources that they need to help them cope with what they're facing and to work through it. I don't think that it's realistic to remove every stressor from their lives, because that's what life is about—facing challenges and growing through them. But I hope that when they face challenges, they know who they can turn to for help and for support and what resources are available out there. So if we can create an atmosphere of being very open to seeking help, not being afraid of being judged or feeling bad that you have an issue, I think that would be the transformation that I hope to see.

MK

Any last words you have for the people who are reading the book itself? To the children who are reading the book, who are out there, fighting their own fights, struggling in their own battles—what would you say to them?

Li Shan

I want to tell them that life is full of challenges. They're there for a reason. So as cliché as it sounds, challenges are there to mould you into becoming a better person, to grow in an area of your life. So don't be afraid to take on the challenge, but don't be afraid to seek help and support when you need it too. Talk to your teachers, talk to your parents, talk to your caregivers.

If I could just give a shout out to the Tinkle Friend helpline—just call the helpline. Chat with them online if you need to. Find an adult who can listen. That's how you will grow. Because challenges are inevitable and life is full of hardships, but I believe that there is a reason why people go through these hardships. It's really to learn a certain lesson that would enable them to grow into a better person and become stronger. So I hope that whoever is reading this won't give up hope if they face challenges or struggles. We all need support. We're not meant to go through this journey alone. So we need to learn how to depend on others and ask for help when we need it.

CHAPTER 10

We Feel What We Feel Because We Feel

By Michelle Koay, High School Counsellor,
St. Joseph's Institution International

Michelle made a career switch from working as an engineer in MINDEF to a counsellor today. She started out volunteering as an SAF Para counsellor and was inspired to embark on a full-time career as a counsellor. She shares about the different layers of stigma in society, and that some mental health conditions, such as depression due to the loss of a loved one, are less stigmatising than others, such as depression due to marital issues. She stresses the importance of learning to treat one another with compassion as we each walk through our own paths to healing.

FROM ENGINEER TO COUNSELLOR

MK

You started out as an engineer before becoming a therapist yourself. What made you decide on the career switch?

Michelle

When I was an engineer, I worked primarily with machines. I realized then that I found it more enriching and enjoyable to work with people instead. I was working in MINDEF[39] at that time and the SAF[40] Counselling Centre (SCC) had a programme for Para counsellors, which was a course for volunteer counsellors. I applied for that course and became an SAF Para counsellor after learning some basic counselling skills. Anyone within the organization who had difficulties could see a para counsellor, so I got the opportunity to work with different groups of people. One opportunity was to interact with detainees from the SAF detention barracks. I met them a few times and after they were released, I followed up for a few more sessions.

All these different experiences made me feel that engineering was probably not for me, so I decided then to switch fields to counselling and do that on a full-time basis.

MK

What was that journey like, especially when counselling in SAF?

Michelle

It was eye-opening. When I was in school, I was very privileged. I come from a reasonably decent background without having to worry about finances and I went to rather good schools. Hence,

---

39 MINDEF: Ministry of Defence

40 SAF: Singapore Armed Forces

I grew up interacting with people with more privileged backgrounds, and there were a lot of things that I did not get to see as I was growing up.

As a counsellor in SCC, I met a range of people—people who lived in one-room flats, those who struggled to make ends meet, people who have taken drugs before, those who experienced domestic violence. I met people from different walks of life, which helped me to be appreciative of what I have and to be able to journey with them.

PUBLIC AWARENESS IS A DOUBLE-EDGED SWORD

MK

When you were working as a counsellor, what were the misconceptions, if any, regarding mental health?

Michelle

When I was growing up, people were not really exposed to knowledge about mental health. There was a lot of taboo and stigma attached to mental health, and many thought that you were crazy if you had some issues with your mental health. In those days, the Institute of Mental Health (IMH) was known as Woodbridge Hospital, and no one wanted to be associated with having to go to Woodbridge Hospital. By the time I went on to do my Master's in counselling and started working as a full-time counsellor, people became more aware about mental health in Singapore. However, there were still concerns around seeing a therapist or counsellor.

MK

As though there is a taboo around it.

Michelle

For sure. At that time, it was not a good thing to acknowledge any kind of weakness. It was a process to change this mindset over time.

I feel that overall, there have been a lot of positive changes in Singapore too. During my volunteer days up until before I became a counsellor, you wouldn't see many articles and much information about mental health. It was usually very *hush hush*. But over time, I noticed that HPB[41], IMH and other agencies began pushing out more content and educational talks that they hadn't been before. For example, Beyond the Label, a very successful campaign by NCSS[42], has provided numerous videos to help people understand mental health issues, combat mental health stigma, and provide information on ways to seek help. It's so good because they make it very accessible to people so that we are able to have those conversations and not feel as if we can only talk about it behind closed doors. I think it is helpful for people to be aware and not scared—otherwise you wouldn't be willing to seek help or accept that something's not quite right.

If I may veer off a little—what I find tricky is that public awareness is a double-edged sword. When you have more information out there, you have more information that is wrong as well. Sometimes, working in a school setting, I realize that young people are a lot more inquisitive and tech savvy. They can access information online, but they cannot discern whether it's right or wrong. Some of them get appropriate and correct information that helps them notice that their friends may not be doing well, and they even take the initiative to accompany them to see the school counsellor or check in with them to see if they're okay.

41 HPB: Health Promotion Board

42 NCSS: National Council of Social Service

But the flip side is they start self-diagnosing, which I think can be problematic, because it is not advisable to use the internet as a resource to self-diagnose. Maybe you notice a couple of things that are not quite right, but you should always speak to a mental health professional or doctor to see what exactly it is about. People tend to pick out certain phrases here and there, which obviously they don't understand, and we'll have to do some guesswork to figure out how much of it is genuinely a problem they've been experiencing, and how much of it is them trying to fulfill their own prophecy. They'll read the information and—

MK

They match themselves.

Michelle

Yes, they'll end up doing that. So that's the challenge there.

A GENERATION OF INFORMATION OVERLOAD

MK

With your experience as a counsellor working with adolescents at Raffles Girls' School and St Joseph's Institution International, what are the emotional and psychological challenges that students face?

Michelle

There is a growing concern about self-harm and suicidal ideation among teenagers today. They are facing a lot of academic pressure from society, their school, peers, parents, and themselves. They think that if they don't do well, it's the end of the world. We have noticed that depression and anxiety is a lot more prevalent among teens.

Some parents and adults may then say, 'Oh last time during my days, we don't have all these problems. Don't know why nowadays the kids can't even deal with all these things. We had to do this, we had to do that. Now we've got helpers and all this, why they still cannot cope?' There are these kinds of questions. But to be fair to this generation of kids, life is a lot more different and a lot more complex these days.

One big factor is that they're exposed to social media and the internet which, in the past, even though we had other kinds of things to deal with, when you are exposed to a whole lot of information, it may not be age-appropriate, which becomes problematic. Let's say they access social media at twelve years old or earlier. They may not necessarily understand what's going on, and there's so much that they are bombarded with that may not be age-appropriate, and so it is hard for them to process. It can actually obviously increase their stress. On top of that, with the way the education system is built, there's a lot expected of them—not just on the academic level, but in their extracurricular activities as well. You also have to make sure your social media is running well. You have to maintain your outward-facing life, your school life, plus your extracurricular activities. So there's quite a lot there that they have to deal with that makes it more challenging for them.

THERAPY 101

MK

Therapy is gaining a lot of popularity in Singapore, but it is still a relatively new term. Could you share with us what it's like going for therapy? Can people really resolve their problems by speaking to another person through therapy processes?

Michelle

I would say *of course can lah.*

There are obviously many different types of therapeutic approaches out there, and I think the most common one is talk therapy. But even those have a variety of modalities. Because generally, suppose if you think about just talking to people, where is that headed to, if you're just chit-chatting? There isn't really a direction. You're just talking for the sake of talking, or maybe you're just talking about an area of interest, or whatever—it's just talking.

But in talk therapy, we try to understand better what's going on in the head, in the heart, or whatever the person may be experiencing. In that setting, if it's safe enough, they'll feel as if they can share a bit more. If, let's say, I don't know you as well, maybe I won't tell you things that would make me feel a bit more vulnerable. Whereas in a therapeutic setting, it's safe, and they would feel okay to open up a little bit more and share something they may not have shared with somebody else. That's when you can process some of these experiences.

MK

What kind of experiences?

Michelle

It really depends on what the person is going through.

MK

Are we dealing with past issues?

Michelle

That may be part of it, but not necessarily.

MK

So it's more of present-time issues?

Michelle

Yes and no. I think what happens is sometimes even if that person comes with a present-day issue, it may be partly linked to something that has happened to them before that is playing out in their present-day life. So if they don't make sense of what has happened before, those things that were undealt with may play out in their present-day life, and that needs to be processed in a way that helps them understand better and make sense of why that happened in their lives, and how come even though it happened so long ago, some remnants may still be playing out in their interaction with other people, how they lead their lives—

MK

Or how they relate with themselves.

Michelle

So it could be any of those things. Basically, that kind of processing would be really helpful, and depending on the kind of modality the therapist conducts, certain strategies can help them unpack things that may not be working out for them. It doesn't mean that it is meant to fix or get rid of their past experiences. In fact, whatever experiences that have happened cannot be erased. That's not the aim of therapy. But everything that has happened to us makes us who we are today, so I wouldn't encourage throwing our past away.

MK

How can we erase our past? It gives us our sense of how we ended up here today. It is what it is. Your greatest strength comes from your experiences. Your greatest weakness also comes from your experiences.

Michelle

Right! So even if a person has had some bad experiences, it is how they make sense of it to move forward and live their lives in a way that is constructive and fulfilling. Because you can have a bad experience and become a very bitter person, but that is unlikely to help you move forward because you are still stuck in that place being bitter and unhappy. You would probably make other people's lives unpleasant because of all that unhappiness and bitterness.

THE LAYERS OF SOCIETAL STIGMA

MK

There are many stigmas in society that prevent people from asking for help. We spoke about that earlier on. In your personal and professional experiences, which do you think are the most prominent stigmas?

Michelle

There are some things that can and cannot be talked about. I would say that if you're talking about mental health topics, whether it's depression or anxiety, those terms are not as stigmatising today, but it depends on what the driving factor or cause is.

For example, suppose the depression is linked to a loss of a loved one. That kind of depression is not as stigmatising, because people have compassion towards it and are able to understand and reach out. The parts that are a lot more difficult to deal with would be linked to things like separation, divorce, or other kinds of marital issues, partly because we don't know how to talk and support the other person through those struggles. We always want families to stick together. So when we see kids being unhappy when their parents are fighting, we don't feel very good, we don't know how to deal with it, and we don't actually recognize that maybe the parent is actually suffering from depression, hence the marital issues.

In a school setting, if the student wasn't able to go to school because of depression and did not finish their education, that tends to be frowned upon. But compare it to somebody who is struggling hard and still takes exams despite their depression—they are seen very differently.

Another factor would be gender. We have a lot more compassion and acceptance towards females experiencing mental health issues, but so much for males. So the acceptance or perpetuation of mental health stigmas largely depends and varies with context. I feel more strongly about this because we tend to be harsher to our boys and men in general, and if they show signs of depression or anxiety, then our response tends to be *you just have to get over it.*

MK

You should not cry.

Michelle

Yes, that's usually the case for them.

MK

Are you familiar with the men's mental health suicide statistics?

Michelle

I think those of us in this field are generally aware that it's a lot higher than females.

But we tend not to reach out to the boys and men who may be struggling emotionally. They also tend to hide it a lot more, and we don't even know that they're struggling, because it's not so acceptable for them to talk about things that aren't going so well.

MK

How do you think we can start reducing some of these stigmas in society today?

Michelle

We need to start having conversations about it. Fortunately, there are more and more people who are beginning to talk about it openly. We even have more practitioners saying 'It's okay, men are also human beings who will experience these emotions as well. How do we help them out?'

One of the interesting things I realized about how men express their emotions is that there's a tendency to allow them to express anger, but not sadness. What happens is that their depression comes out in terms of anger, aggressive and bad behaviour, and so on. But if you process a bit more, you might realize that the person is suffering from depression or some mental health issues.

MK

There are layers underneath the anger they show on the surface.

Michelle

So sometimes we misunderstand it, and we ask the guys 'Why are you so rude? Why are you so aggressive and angry at all of us?' But that's probably also because they don't know how to make sense of their own anger and understand what's underneath that anger. This is something our society needs to work on—to equip our boys with the emotional lingo and normalise and validate their feelings, so that they can express them in more appropriate ways.

MK

It's the same thing—we've been trained in schools how to use our brain, but no one ever taught us how to use our heart to feel. We don't understand that emotions have layers. Happiness is not everything, yet people chase after it as though it is. But you know, we've got to realize that without the duality of things—without sadness, how would we be able to appreciate what happiness is? If we're feeling happy every day, that's a constant state, and not happiness anymore.

Michelle

I was talking to a student about emotions. Sometimes we think that you can only have one emotion at a time, but it is possible to have several emotions at the same time, and there are different levels of intensity for each emotion as well.

MK

You can feel happy and angry and sad at the same time.

Michelle

And after that, we talked about the movie *Inside Out*. Initially, all of them had the different memory balls of a single colour. But later on in the film, there were memory balls with a mixture of colours, so there's happiness and sadness in the same memory ball. Our emotions are not necessarily expressed in discrete variables.

IT'S LIKE WORKING IN A COAL MINE

MK

What are some struggles you face as a mental health professional that people do not usually know about?

Michelle

Well, in this field, because we take on quite a bit of the stories that people come with, it's like working in a coal mine. You go to the mine, day in, day out. By the time you're out, you will be covered in coal dust. In that sense, once you're in this field, you have to make sure that there's a way for you to also shake off this coal dust whenever you do the work that you need to do. So that's the part that is a risk that we have to realize as practitioners in the field. If we don't take care of ourselves, we may actually fall into the same patterns as the people we treat, because sometimes we may relate or over-empathise.

It's back to the double-edged sword. You need to be really empathic to empathise with somebody, but then you run the risk of over-empathizing and affecting yourself as well. So those are the things we need to be more aware of—that sometimes there's only so much emotional baggage we can deal with, and it can be quite difficult, especially if your client has tons of it. So having to take care of those different aspects is really important.

MK

What do you think about drawing boundaries? Being able to have the clarity and awareness to say that 'This is my client's issue. My issues are my issues. I can only own my issues—I can't own my client's issues'.

Michelle

One example of clear boundaries which we have to set is that we shouldn't have dual relationships. That means that for a client, we see them only in sessions, and after that, we do not associate with them in any way. So we shouldn't call them out for coffee or lunch.

But in terms of how it affects us, we are all human beings. Actually, with human emotions, you almost cannot draw lines! It is nearly impossible. As long as you are in this field, you will be affected by the client. What's more important is that you are able to make sense of what's going on and be able to process and discern whether it is your own issue or your client's issue, or your client's issues triggering your own issues. If that happens, then of course you go and deal with it. Or it could even be your own issue triggering the client's issues. It could work in many many ways, but it's really about being a lot more aware of what's going on in the here and now, and then processing it. Because what may happen is that, let's say I'm working with a particular client and I feel a certain way. It's legitimate that my feelings are going to be valid, and sometimes my feelings and emotions inform me about what may be going on with the client as well. So in that sense, I cannot strictly draw the so-called boundaries.

MK

I totally can relate to that. I asked the question partly because I know a lot of caregivers struggle with it, from my limited experience. I think that was very nice in terms of how you put that into perspective. Being able to be in the present moment is really important too.

Michelle

One final point to put across is my hope for the community to become more genuinely connected with one another. I feel that disconnection is one of the primary causes of mental health issues. If we take the time to care for one another, and reach out to others, we will feel less isolated and alone, and this will make it easier for us to cope when we are faced with challenges in our lives.

CHAPTER 11

Fresh To The Scene, Ready To Make A Difference

By Amirah Munawwarah, Registered Art Therapist

Graduating from the art therapy programme in 2020, Amirah talks about her interest in making a difference to people through art therapy, and her experience as a budding art therapist in the scene. She reflects that while her generation of people are still relatively quiet about mental health issues, the current generation is much more vocal about it. Though we are beginning to talk about mental health issues more openly today, much more work still needs to be done for society at large to accept people with mental health conditions.

WORKING ON THE GROUND

MK

What got you interested in mental health issues and why did you decide to pursue art therapy?

Amirah

It began when I was sixteen, in Secondary four, when we were choosing our polytechnic courses. That's when I started to notice how individuals had different reactions to the same collective events and experiences. It got me thinking *what's going on? How and why is it that my experiences and perspectives are different from my friends?* That's how psychology came in and I furthered my studies in it. I knew from the start that I wanted to go for a master's programme, but I wasn't sure which branch of psychology to specialize in. I decided to take some time after my bachelor's degree to go for volunteering opportunities instead of just jumping into any field, considering that a master's programme was going to be very specialized. I didn't want to waste two years of my life doing or studying something that I wasn't interested in.

I volunteered at the Riding for the Disabled Association (RDA), and it was a first-hand experience working with a group of children with autism for the first time. Seeing them progress in about eight sessions made me realize that I wanted to do therapy work instead of doing backend work. Thinking about how I could put all this knowledge together was how I found art therapy.

MK

I also saw on your website that people use art therapy for things like finding their purpose and searching for the meaning of life. These are major questions. How do you think they are related to mental health, and why do you think people have to look into them?

Amirah

That's a particular area that I'm very interested in, and what I looked into for my master's thesis. Growing up, when I took public transport, I wondered why everyone looked 'dead', as if there's no life in them when they go to work. That was a pivotal moment when purpose and meaning in life came into picture, where I told myself *I don't want to end up like that. I want to wake up and feel that there's something to life.*

But after a while, when you meet friends and relatives, especially when you've just graduated, you start getting questions like *what's your job? What are you going to do?* And these questions are usually intertwined with things like finances or family expectations. But a lot of times, we forget to ask *what do I want to do in life*? Mid-career changes typically stem from *this is not what I want to do* so it always comes back to identity. It's just something that we don't really look into too often. We just think that *we can do this later.* If you have those dreams, you'll always say *I'll do it next year or when I have enough resources*, but when would that be, exactly?

GRADUATING DURING A PANDEMIC

MK

Could you share about how it was like graduating from your Masters in 2020 during the pandemic? How do you think COVID has affected society's understanding of mental health?

Amirah

I graduated during the Circuit Breaker.[43] Some of my classmates and I feel that we have not graduated yet because there wasn't a proper closure. We were suddenly taken away from class,

[43] Circuit Breaker refers to the three-month nationwide lockdown in Singapore to curb the spread of COVID-19

taken away from the graduation ceremony, from our belongings that we left in school. Speaking from personal experience and reflections, it's the quarantine aspect that allowed individuals to think about mental health rather than the pandemic itself. The effect of the coronavirus pandemic itself on our mental health manifests itself through physical symptoms like fevers, runny nose, and et cetera.

During quarantine, we were taken away from a lot of things that we were used to and enjoy. So even though we're quarantined with our family members, partners, or housemates that we can still socialise with, it's still very different because we're now confined to this limited physical space, and anything and everything we want to do has to be in there. That was when people tried to think *what can I do in this space that can reflect the outside world, somehow?*

Singapore did come into Circuit Breaker slightly later than other countries, so we got to read information and news about how people from other countries were dealing with their own lockdown issues, like anxiety and depression, which were starting to rise. I wouldn't say we were mentally prepared, but we were slightly aware of it. And when we were in lockdown itself, that's when everyone started to think *okay, this is what we can do.* So, in a way, it helped to boost mental health awareness.

It's a good and a bad thing that the pandemic and lockdown happened. I don't know how else mental health can be brought up if there's no pandemic. Other mental health issues then started coming up, like self-care, self-love, suicide, depression, and self-harm. It's been ongoing for so many years, but there wasn't much done or talked about until everyone was in the pandemic lockdown.

TAKING IT FROM THEORY TO APPLICATION

MK

I know that you had been working as an educator for six years before pursuing your master's in art therapy. What was the experience like for you, and what are some of the challenges that you noticed children faced?

Amirah

My educator stint was conducting weekend classes. It just so happened that my centre had a lot of students coming from challenging backgrounds. I've had a student with autism, one with ADHD[44], and those living with foster families. I was only in my second and third year of studying for my psychology degree then. It was challenging because I didn't have the experience to manage those students. There were only one to two challenging students in a class size of twelve, but still, not having that knowledge and experience to work with them can disrupt how we teach the rest.

One of the students had ADHD. He was only eight or nine. It was still manageable at that time, but it was tough in the sense that I had to work with him weekly. So that was when I started to think—I was studying psychology, but theory-wise it wasn't something I could apply. I really needed to learn how to apply the theories, the real work. I can read about ADHD and read a lot of books but—

MK

But none of that really works if you can't apply it and help people.

Amirah

Yeah! It was the application part that got me thinking.

TRACING BACK TO CHILDHOOD

MK

A part of mental health is also about addressing our childhood traumas. How does childhood trauma affect our mental health as adults?

[44] ADHD: Attention-deficit/hyperactivity disorder

Amirah

Most people tend to either forget or dismiss childhood traumas, but they do affect us one way or another, positively or negatively. How you are right now is partly a result of how you were raised. How you see things can also be a result of how you were taught to view the world.

I like to compare childhood relationships with our parents to how stray dogs or cats interact with people. It is the same way the kittens follow their mum. If the mummy cat interacts well with people, the kitten will do so too. But, if the mummy cat is afraid of people, the kittens tend to follow as well. If the mum is a quiet person, usually the child will be quiet. I see it in my family too. I have a very social dad and a very introverted mum, so there's a balance. And when I look at my neighbours who have both introverted parents—

MK

You start seeing the difference in the permutations.

Amirah

Their children can either be introverts too, or they can socialise. That's the part where you decide to do what you want to do. People always say that they want to forget their childhood, but it manifests differently in various forms, and you don't notice that it is coming from your childhood.

MK

How can people start developing a sense of awareness so they know the triggers and reactions they might have towards the world?

Amirah

It comes down to whether you want to become more self-aware. A lot of times, people deny. I have friends who deny their past, saying that 'These things aren't happening because of my childhood'.

But from hearing their stories, it is rather apparent how it relates and manifests. If the person rejects or denies whatever they're going through, there's not much you can do except be there until they're willing to take the first step forward. I learned that I cannot take the first step for them. What I can do is be there as a friend, but there's also a risk as you might end up feeling burnt out, which is something I had to learn the hard way because I wanted to help my friends. I wanted them to go for counselling, but after a while, I'm the one who's burnt out. So I had to put my boundaries in place to know that *this is what I can do, and if this does not happen, it's not on me, because I've been trying.* But I do tell them that if you need anything or if you need someone, I'll still be there.

It's not easy to tell someone to suddenly raise their awareness. I personally find that it has to start with gentle approaches. We can't go to the person and force them to go to counselling or therapy. It doesn't work that way. Based on my personal experiences, gentle and soft approaches like talking about it, asking them about the issue, or giving some suggestions if they ask, might help them. Sometimes they ask me do you think I should go for therapy? And I say yeah, you should—I am seeing a therapist too. But after a while, they tend to forget that thought. It only came to them in that moment.

MK

There was no commitment to it.

Amirah

That's when I realized I can only do so much. If you don't take that first step, I can only do so much.

THERE'S STILL A LONG ROAD AHEAD OF US

MK

As a freshly graduated art therapist, what are some hopes you have for mental health in Singapore?

Amirah

At this point in time, mental health is getting more recognition and people are talking about self-care, self-love, and all those things that are related to mental health. But there's still some hesitance when we talk about mental health issues like self-harm and suicide. Those are things that I would say the general public is still not ready to talk about. In a way, we are only looking at the positive aspects like self-care and self-love. It's very nice and flowery. But when we talk about suicide and self-harm, it becomes a very hard topic that not everyone can talk about and we still get comments like *don't tell this to other people, keep it quiet, it will pass*, and all these other things that don't really help, that can be more harmful than helpful. So, I'm really hoping that through various approaches like art therapy, or even talking and having discussions about mental health concerns, we can slowly start to open up to talk about these hard topics like suicide, self-harm, depression, and anxiety.

I find that the younger generation is very different now. My generation was very quiet about it, but the current generation is really outspoken. So hopefully generations can teach other generations. But even then, the other generations have to be open to accept it as well.

Well, actually even those who are in my generation are still influenced by the older generations. Speaking on a cultural level, there are people who say that if you are religious and spiritual, you won't have all these concerns. I can see that these things were carried forward from their parents.

I have a friend, the same age as me, who just had her first child, and she was talking about how she shouldn't feel sad. From psychological knowledge, we know that it might be postpartum depression, but she denied it and she was even afraid to feel sad because her parents and her sisters told her that she couldn't feel sad, because she has God. That's how I realized that these mindsets are still occurring in our generation, even though what my friend is going through is a very natural process. As a woman, when you go through pregnancy and birth, it's a total change. Living in a family that doesn't allow you to speak up—

MK

Creates another problem. You can't express yourself for who you are.

Amirah

I guess even if she did express, it would be dismissed, like *you shouldn't say that, you have God, you have this and that.* It was not the help or treatment she needed at that point in time.

MK

That's an interesting personal account.

Amirah

It's these personal accounts that allowed me to reflect and to observe that such issues are still happening, that this is not talked about. Even just dealing with multiple perspectives is hard for some people. They will insist that 'My perspective is the only correct one, yours is not'. This is something that's still ongoing. There is definitely much more that needs to be done at this point in time. We have come quite a long way, and there's still a long way ahead of us too.

CHAPTER 12

Early Years Lay The Foundation

By Ng Gim Choo, Founder, The EtonHouse Group

The early years form the most important period in a child's development. Children model after the people around them. Their mindset and attitudes are shaped by their experiences in their environment, and that will likely determine how they view the world as they grow up. Parents have the responsibility to reflect on the kind of influence they have on their children, and create an environment where their children can grow up with confidence and resilience.

SETTING UP ETONHOUSE: A SCHOOL THAT RESPECTS CHILDREN AND TEACHERS

Gim Choo

My husband had the opportunity to work in the UK and I decided that I should spend my time with the family, so I resigned to follow him to the UK to become a full-time housewife for nearly 14 years. In England, my daughter *loved* going to school. On the weekends, she would put on her uniform, excited to go to school. When I told her school was closed on weekends, she was so disappointed!

In Singapore, she didn't want to go to school. Once, her teacher asked her to colour a flower red, but she loved morning glories, so she coloured it purple, and she was scolded. Next, the teacher instructed her to write the word 豆, and that has seven Chinese strokes. She said it was too difficult, so she didn't want to go to school. So I kept her at home, and hoped she would change her mind the following week, but who knew? She still didn't want to go to school! And when I went to school to organise the withdrawal procedures, the principal scolded me and said 'I don't understand. Why is it that other children can follow instructions, but your daughter can't? And as a mother, you are not supportive at all, you kept your daughter at home! So for that reason, we are not going to refund your deposit'. I said 'Fine, fine, I respect whatever decision'.

But in the UK, school was so different. I think it was the respect she got from the school, and that made learning so much more fun for her. When we came back to Singapore, she only wanted that type of school, but that did not exist. That inspired me to set up EtonHouse. There was also a lot of encouragement from my husband and my brother. Family support was very important.

Support from the children's families is also very important. The stress is not only from managing the staff, but also from managing parents. When parents send a child to you, they expect you to perform miracles. And some parents do not treat our staff well. Once, a parent used the four-letter-word to scold our teachers. The teacher was so devastated that I told the parents that in school, we talk about respect, and we cannot allow a parent to use such rude words towards our teachers. And I said 'We need you to apologise to our teachers', but he refused. So I said 'It would be very difficult for us to work together and with your child, perhaps it's good for you to start looking for other schools'. So they started looking for other schools but could not find one. And the mother said, 'How could you, because of adult issues, let my child suffer? These are issues amongst the adults. I said yeah, if you did something that led your child to suffer, you should apologise, then we can move on'. But the husband wouldn't, and eventually, the child left the school.

Dealing with all this is very very painful. Parents want the best, and the teachers get the stress from the parents and grandparents. It's a very very demanding job in our profession. In fact, we always feel that the teachers enjoy working with children, but it is the parenting pressure, the pressure from the customers that makes a lot of teachers just go 'I've had enough. I want to leave the profession'. It's very sad that in Singapore, we have trained many many teachers, and a lot of people have even switched their jobs to go into early childhood education, but not many stay. A lot of teachers always talk about how nice it would be if they only had children and no parents to deal with. That's the pressure we get working in that profession. We don't have assets. Our assets are our teachers. We always say teachers are very important to us. We want to reduce their stress, and help teachers to understand what stresses them, and to work with them. Because if the teachers' wellbeing is addressed, I think they can contribute their best.

BUILDING RESILIENCE IN CHILDREN

MK

Got it. As an education system, how can we prepare children to be more ready to handle larger circumstances that are bigger than them? Because oftentimes, when we talk about mental health collapsing, it is because they are dealing with something they're not ready for and because of that, they don't have the resilience to push through.

Gim Choo

I always feel it's the confidence level. Some children do not appear very confident. For example, when I go to the school, some five-year-old children will ask me, 'Who are you? Why did you come here to visit the school? Or how may I help you?' Some others, who are also five years old, will give no eye contact. They're so frightened! They'll walk away, and they won't even want to talk to me. Perhaps it is partly because we tell children not to talk to strangers, but I think in the Asian context, we tend to have a top-down approach. So without any instructions, children may not be very sure of what to do, and they may feel insecure.

MK

Kids model after their parents. So how parents carry themselves, whether it's in a conscious or unconscious way, does have a huge impact on the kid.

Gim Choo

That's why I thought early childhood education is very important. In the early years, their personalities are formed. So if they're expected to be confident, it sort of moulds their characters—

MK

Correct. It goes all the way, years down the road. And that's why when I knew what EtonHouse actually does, I figured that you probably know something about this whole domain.

Gim Choo

And then a lot of people ask, 'Why would I want to spend money on early years?'

[MK sighs heavily]

Gim Choo

I always tell them that the early years lay the foundation. By four years old, their personalities are formed, and there's very little you can do, so it's better to invest a lot of resources when they're young. So there's this boy who has Tourette syndrome, and people don't really understand . . . Imagine this—someone told him, 'You should explain your syndrome to your classmates'. And he did. He said 'I explained to my classmates, but they still didn't talk to me. They laughed at me, then I made a choice not to be their friend'.

He became more confident after the doctor told him it's a disease. He opened up more and talked to his classmates. So I think it's internally what you feel about the stigma. If you've always felt diffident, but you choose to adopt a mindset that 'It's okay that I have this, this is who I am' when you open up to others, you become confident. People laugh, but you're not going to bother about it. It's how you think. Nobody can influence you. Let people laugh, so long as you have a strong sense of self.

DEALING WITH THE SUICIDE OF CHILDREN

[MK is playing the I Feel You[45] video trailer]

MK

These are the artworks. So you know, instead of doing the traditional painting itself—

Gim Choo

These are real?

MK

Yeah. They're all strangers who just met each other for ten minutes.

Gim Choo

And what did you ask of them?

MK

To talk about anything. Their personal truth. And then stories of losses, grief, anger, and existential crisis started showing up.

Peimin

This was for . . . Is this linked to your suicide prevention movement?

MK

Yeah, it's one of the works that I created deliberately.

---

[45] 'I Feel You' is a socially engaged participatory artwork produced by ThisConnect in 2020 that involves ten pairs of strangers who hold each other's hands to connect while sharing their deep-seated stories of pain, loss, and vulnerability. Each person is given ten minutes to share. When one person speaks, the other party holds the space and only responds with one sentence: 'I feel you.'

Gim Choo

This sort of death, you need closure. So my friend's son committed suicide. She felt, *how come I didn't know my son had depression and wanted to commit suicide?* So the day she went to work, I think the son closed the door, switched on the gas, and committed suicide. And her family didn't allow her to go back to the flat and attend her son's funeral, so she never got to say goodbye to him. I think her family wanted to protect her, but she never got closure. She never got to say goodbye. So she went into depression for a couple of years, and she always thinks about *why. Why didn't I know my son went into depression and wanted to commit suicide?* Even up till today, because she has two boys, when people ask, 'What happened to your elder son?' She doesn't know what to say.

You could just say he's away travelling or something. But one of my other friends, whose son also committed suicide, said that one thing that helped him is to always think that his son overseas—but I don't know whether he's lying to himself or not. I don't know, is that the right way?

MK

Well, people always say that time heals all wounds, but we know that it's not true. The people who are suffering in those states know that they can't move on.

Gim Choo

So how do you move on? Because the son committed suicide! The son lost money, wanted to get money from him, and he said 'No, I cannot always save you, you have to sort out yourself', and the son just committed suicide. So he says *I think he's away* to make himself feel better.

PARENTING IS A CONSCIOUS EFFORT

MK

Is there any message you would like to say to the world?

Gim Choo

(laughing) I think bringing up children is a responsible task. And we have to reflect on ourselves. Certain percentage of our behaviour is from our father, certain percentage of behaviour is from our mother, our grandmothers, and so on. We are very much influenced by them.

MK

Yes!

Gim Choo

So I was talking about caregivers, parents, and grandparents. Make a conscious and consistent effort. Because usually children are very smart, very clever. If I don't get something from my mother, I'll get it from my father. I just need to cry and cry, and somebody will give me attention. So I think it's a conscious consistent effort—

MK

On the parent's part. Because parents have the role and responsibility to nurture their child.

Gim Choo

I just feel that, don't compare. Don't compare your children. Don't say 'Your brother is good at this'. Don't compare your children with your friend's children. Don't compare your children with older children. You know every child is different, unique, so don't compare. You also cannot compare your husband! Having chosen the husband, he's the best husband you can ever have. You don't go and compare and say 'My friend's husband is so good, you know?' How would the man feel? And similarly, don't go and compare your wife to your friend's wife and say 'Why do you treat me so badly?' Don't compare! (laughing) Before you get married, just open your eyes and choose the right person and after you get married, that's it.

MK

Thank you.

Gim Choo

That's what I told my son on their wedding day.
[laughter]

CHAPTER 13

The Difference Educators Can Make

By Mysara, Caregiver, Caregivers Alliance Limited

Mysara cared for her father when he became ill, and it was only after he passed away had she noticed the extent to which her third son had grown attached to him. Her father's death had a left a huge impact on her son's upbringing and mental health through the different stages of his life. Today, Mysara continues to support her son through his mental health recovery, and hopes that her story will encourage more parents to be involved and observant of what their children are going through so that they can reach out and extend a lifeline when it is needed the most.

IT HURT WHEN I DIDN'T UNDERSTAND WHAT MY SON WAS GOING THROUGH

MK

What made you decide to become a caregiver?

Mysara

The first person I was taking care of was my late father. When he fell sick, he chose to be with me because my first boy was his first grandchild. After he passed, that's when I found out that my third son was very attached to him. When he was living with me, my third son was always with him, so my husband didn't really need to take care of him, and we were ignorant about a lot of things. That was when my third son was about five.

So I didn't think much about that even though I'm in the education field. I teach people about things, I was conscious about sibling rivalries, about the stages of birth, but I wasn't really paying attention to my third son. I only noticed when my father passed on and my third son was affected very badly. And even still, we didn't pay much attention because he didn't make a lot of noise. Even at five years old, he was very clever. He had a stack of those battery-operated cars, and my father was the one who would keep stock. One day, my younger brother came, and my son said 'Uncle, can you make sure the battery does not finish? Please replenish the battery'. I think he thought of my father. 'Now that dada's not around, who's gonna replenish my battery?' That part saddens me, when I look back now, at all those days I ignored him. He would come to my room every night, stand at the door, and not make any noise. Actually, I feel sad when I speak about this because I didn't think much of it then. He had to cope with so many things.

Later on when he started his temper tantrums, my husband couldn't cope, and my son abused himself quite badly because he would lie down on the floor and start kicking the door, and we had to replace it. And one door was $100 and there was a ton I had to replace—almost $600—and still, we were not worried about him! We were worried about the cabinet because we didn't have much. We were running our own centre, we were worried about money, and thought he was just being naughty.

MK

Where is he now?

Mysara

He's not at home. He's twenty-five now, serving NS[46]. So now when I look back, I try to understand things that I overlooked. These are the things we didn't see back when he was in Primary Six. He truly played up at school. He's a smart boy and he's an artist.

He's very gentle inside. So emotional. That's why teachers make a lot of difference. In Secondary Two, one good Malay teacher saw the talent in him then asked him to draw a mural in the Malay class. So he drew. I was surprised when I saw the black rose and said 'Tariq did that?' He was only fourteen! So he drew on the wall every day and when I came to see him, I couldn't believe that the small drawing being transferred to the wall was so good. When the teacher saw this, he got better. He joined the orchestra, and he did very well. No musical background, but he got into the main band. But when he was in the main band, he got bullied because some of the seniors were not happy. When we

---

[46] NS: National Service

went to the Victoria Concert Hall, bad things happened to him. He was so happy because I was coming to watch him play a solo, *Fly Me To The Moon.* He practiced and every day I listened to him. And when it was his turn to do the solo, we all waited, but nothing happened. They let the senior play instead. And later on in life, he told me that actually during Secondary 1 and 2, Mummy, every day after school, I will go and sniff glue'.

(Mysara begins to cry) It hurt me that I didn't know my son was sniffing glue, and I was here doing nothing. I didn't know. And he was very angry during that time. More cabinets got broken. That's when he started punching because he couldn't talk and he couldn't express himself. When I say it's time to go to school, he says 'I don't want, I don't want!' Then we'll go crazy. 'Why don't want?! I don't want!' Then bang here, bang there. So we tried to get the teacher's help, but when the school called me, I also didn't know how to help him. I said 'What's wrong with you?' Later on, we found out that he had been bullied a few times. That's the thing—he couldn't express when he did something wrong. He just jammed up. That made things difficult, and he lived in that kind of fear, anger, and he gave us trouble in that way—we thought he was giving us trouble but when he was in trouble, he didn't know how to express it.

To start off, he's very intelligent, very smart, very creative, into arts, and can do a lot of things with his hands. So he tried for Talent Academy[47] again, and there's one course on product design that he could take, but he had to sit for an interview. He didn't pass the first interview because when the interviewer asked him what happened when he was in Secondary Three and Four —there were no results in his report book, nothing—again, he couldn't talk. (getting emotional) He couldn't even say anything,

---

[47] Talent Academy: School of the Arts' (SOTA) Direct School Admissions (DSA) platform

so he just jammed up down there—that's the weakness! Every time you confront him, he can't answer you, so he's out. The second time round, I happened to be at ITE[48] and I happened to know the head there. So I just mentioned that my son wanted to join visual communications, but he couldn't, because of his grades. I told her the problem with him, and she said 'Ask him to apply again'. Again, the teacher made that difference. 'Ask him to apply again. I'll be in there for the interview'. Great, right? This person said 'I'll be sitting in the interview, I'll look out for your son'. Because of luck again, this lady sat there and asked him to make five paper cranes to bring to the interview. I was telling my husband, 'If he's not doing it, he's not interested, so don't bother'. And in the morning when we woke him up, I said 'Do you have your paper cranes? If not then is okay, no need to go'. Then he said (shouting) 'I've done it lah!' He shouted—I was so happy when he said that! So when he came back, I said 'You think you can get in this time?' He said 'Yeah, the lady took my paper cranes'. I said oh, really? All five? 'No, mine was a mobile'. Overnight, he actually turned it into a mobile. He bent wires because even though he was asked to do five paper cranes, he turned it into a mobile! So I said 'One day maybe you can make one for mummy'. Later on I said 'But you never asked for paper, do you have paper to do it?' He said no. I was shocked! His actually tore his drawings and made the mobile out of his own portfolio. As a mother it's like, 'Eh, your drawing, you know? That's your drawing, your beautiful drawing? What?!' Then he talked to me and said 'It's okay, it's my drawing, mummy. I can always do it again'.

Then—amazing. At ITE, things went very well, and again, it was how the teacher approached him. And he is a perfectionist.

---

[48] ITE: Institute of Technical Education

When things are not done properly, he won't submit. The teacher said that during his art exam, half an hour before time's up, he crumpled the whole thing and did it all over again. And of course he couldn't do it in time, right? So he failed. So I told the ITE teacher about this and the ITE teacher was so good about it. Every time he did the final draft, the teacher said 'Give that to me', and the teacher would keep it in case he couldn't do the final in time. The last draft would be very good already. Do you know how good that is? You see, the teacher makes the difference, right? So that's why I want to do research about what teachers can do to turn everything around.

So he did well, got direct entry into polytechnic, but polytechnic killed him again. He became very angry and frustrated. During group assignments, he couldn't manage with other kids, most of whom were younger than him because he skipped school. And that's where he crumbled again, and he started taking substances. I could see that he struggled to finish school. In his second year, he got into trouble. He was at a very low point already, but he had a very good mentor there. And that mentor did tell me that people like him probably could not fit well in this kind of school. What put him down was because he couldn't get up every morning, he would come in a bit late and be considered absent. And he sometimes submitted his assignments late. He said 'Mummy, no point I do anything, because I will still get the lowest. I cannot get an A, whatever good work I do'. That system is the one that killed him, so he thought, *why bother?* He still wanted to do his work, but he had to repeat one module. That's when he started to drink, got in trouble with the law, and got caught.

Only then did the lawyer ask me to get him diagnosed. Only then, we knew . . . Because the private psychiatrist diagnosed him with major depression since he was five. And it cost us a bomb—over $3000 for the diagnosis. But I'm okay, because I get to know what he's suffering from. But the fortnight treatment is too much, like ten minutes would cost $100 over. (getting emotional) He gets upset because he's very sensitive and he always doesn't want us to suffer because of him, so he said 'Mummy, it's okay, I can manage. I promise you I'll be okay again'. Growing up through primary and secondary school, he already started showing signs. And like what one of our counsellors at CAL says, you have to tell people. We cannot know everything. People like me also won't necessarily know. Sometimes I feel so sorry for parents who really don't know much, who don't have knowledge, or have no education. I would do anything for my children but I didn't know, so I didn't do anything. After I got his diagnosis, it became very hard on us. The worst was when he was going through all these court cases, up down up down during school days, then towards the end just before he served the sentence, he knew he was gonna go in. (crying) He asked me this, 'Is it okay if I quit?' At that point in my life, his schooling was not important anymore. *Not important.* I know my son is smart, I know my son is reading every day, he has got good knowledge. That particular paper that you can get as a diploma, that is nothing to me. So I said 'quit', because I didn't want to add any more stress to him. Because at that point in my life, if I could have my son, I didn't care what he's doing anymore. I just wanted him to be there and I'm happy already. That was all. I changed my attitude.

BRING YOURSELF BACK TO LOVE

MK

How did that experience shape the way you look at mental health and mental illness?

Mysara

To me it's like, based on my son, if you're more observant, a lot of things can be helped. And I feel that if you have very good relationships and you build rapport, you can have more conversations. The fact that my son didn't talk to anybody, suffered in silence, and we took it wrongly . . . I feel that there's nothing to be ashamed of at all. My son's not *bad.* It's just that he got into trouble with the police officer and verbally assaulted them when he's not himself. He's sick. Not that he stole or raped somebody! He was sick, and we didn't know. But nobody cares—people just see him as bad. Try to look at the person from their shoes. And I feel that if someone is sick, you need to have treatment. Now, if somebody has cancer, it's okay. But if somebody has mental health problems, it's not okay. If I'm sick, I suffer a heart attack, everybody will be caring towards me. But if I say that I have mental health issues, people get scared, I feel that they don't know how to react. I think that's the main issue.

MK

Got it. And how do you think we can raise awareness of that?

Mysara

I feel that we have brought up a lot of awareness, like in schools, but sometimes it's not easy to look at mental health from the heart. It's always from the rules. For example, if I come to a school counsellor saying 'I have this ideation about suicide', straightaway the principal will be called, everybody will be called, parents will be called, and then everybody goes a little crazy, especially parents. And I'm like, 'Next time I better not tell because these things will happen'. But I feel that even at the professional level, when you make a big fuss about somebody saying *I thought of killing myself,* they will just say 'Next time I better keep quiet and just rot somewhere'.

I think even at CAL[49], I'm connected to those people who are so genuine, who have already been through things. As they

[49] CAL: Caregivers Alliance Limited

say, if you've never stepped into my shoes, don't teach me how to tie my laces. And people have been telling me a lot of things when I was going through those difficulties. 'Oh, maybe you're not strict enough with him or maybe you're too soft, too gentle'. I said I did *everything*! (frustratedly) I was soft, I was gentle, I went crazy, I shouted, I screamed, I went to see all the counsellors, I went to the family service centre because maybe I have that awareness about counselling, but I had no money, so I went for the free one. I went to the school, I talked to the principal, and the principal asked me to send him to the juvenile court. And we sent him there. And the best thing that happened—again, the counsellor there was good. After interviewing him, the counsellor said 'There's nothing wrong with him, why did you bring him here? He's a good boy'. But because they supposed he was bad, he had to be sent to the Boys' Home. Then the director of the Singapore Children's Society, she was good. She woke us up and told us that my son is okay, he's a good boy. Maybe it was how we managed. We didn't talk about how he lost my father then.

MK

Yeah, it started a long time ago.

Mysara

Yeah, and good thing he didn't go into juvenile court. Because you know what would happen to him if he went into the home? He would just go down and go down and go down. So it's good teachers, good people that brought him up—

MK

People who can make a difference.

Mysara

Counselling helped. One thing I remember that the counsellor told me is this: think of a beautiful thing about your child that is something you remember. What beautiful thing do you remember about your son? Is there any item that comes to mind? I said yellow boot, because he's always outdoors playing. That yellow boot reminds me of the beautiful boy he was. So the counsellor said 'He's the same boy here, just that the facade is different'. But because of the temper and swearing, sometimes you want to be away from him. So I keep on thinking of that and bringing myself back into loving him again.

MK

Nice. What is a message you want people out there to know?

Mysara

. . . When my son was in IMH[50], somebody just came to me, and she's just the supervisor of HDB cleaners. She said come, I buy you lunch. I said I cannot eat. She said 'COME, and have something to eat. How can you take care of your son when you're like this?' It woke me up again. That's why I said we have to take care of ourselves. I pull myself up again and again because I want to take care of my son. I've got three others and a husband to take care of, and nobody can be neglected just because of one person. And my son keeps on reminding me, *mummy it's okay, I'll be okay* and he promises to be good.

And professionals can make mistakes. When my son was in the ICU after he attempted to take his own life, the A&E doctor said 'I think your son is on drugs. I think he's on heroin or

[50] IMH: Institute of Mental Health (Singapore's only hospital dedicated to mental health)

something'. I said how do you know? I was very angry because I was scared when the doctor said that to me. I said 'What, my son is on heroin?' And then that very day, a police officer came to me and said there's no evidence he was using drugs. But later on, we found that he actually took all his medication plus alcohol and one bottle of codeine. *He meant to do it.*

[heavy silence]

Mysara

Again, it's a good accident because when he was there, I saw another lady sitting down there quietly until somebody came and said 'He's so young, he's so young!' Then I saw they brought her to another room with an army uniform wrap.

I was just grateful that my son is still there. I don't know what's going to happen to him, but at this moment, I still have him. So I think gratitude is very important. And seeing things around you, noticing them. I think that pulled me up, and again, count your blessings. So now, thank god my son's been out from medication. Ever since the Circuit Breaker[51], he went haywire. He started saying 'I don't want to take medication' abruptly and I was crying, saying 'Please take a bit'. But he said 'No, mummy, I don't want to. Medication makes me mad'.

MK

Yeah . . .

Mysara

Sometimes you never know. You might go through depression, but not all the way down.

[51] Circuit Breaker refers to the three-month nationwide lockdown in Singapore to curb the spread of COVID-19

I went for a course to be a trainer at CAL. After these two to three years, I went through anxiety and panic attacks because they talked about suicide. The lecturer said if I was uncomfortable, I didn't have to do it, but I said I was okay. So I shared, and I was so calm sharing about what my son did but after one night, I felt this pain. Then second night, I ended up in the A&E because one of the questionnaires asked: if people attempt suicide several times, they might just die of suicide. True or false? I was saying 'False false false', *sekali*[52] the answer is true! Straightaway, I went crazy. I was thinking, he did attempt a few times . . . What's going to happen? So now, I have to live with this.

MK

It becomes part of a history that you have to live with.

Mysara

Yeah. I tell myself that I must be positive. Because certain things are beyond our control. My psychiatrist did say that 'Love conquers all'. We do our best as a caregiver, but sometimes, we just wouldn't know, right? My son told me 'It's not easy to live, because mummy, you don't know how painful it is. It's so painful, mummy. It's hard to live. But to die is also very hard'. So I said, 'Why is it hard to die?' He said 'If I were to die, what would happen to you? You have to face all these people. People will start questioning you'.

Then I told him: If anything happened to you, I will miss you for the rest of my life. I'll miss you all the way. Nothing can heal that. That's all, but there's nothing I can do if you decide on this because you told me what you're going to do.

But I also become crazy. Every night I'll check, *is he doing it? Is he doing it? Is he doing it?* But after a while, I let it go when I saw

---

[52] Sekali: A Malay term expressing the notion of 'what if'

him getting better. He told me I have to believe. 'Don't worry, I'll take care of myself. Don't worry, mummy'. Even though sometimes I see he's a bit edgy, I always say 'If there's anything, talk to mummy, okay?' I always tell him to remember that 'We all love you so much. We'll be very sad if anything happens to you'.

MK

I wish you all the best.

CHAPTER 14

Creating A Youth-Led Mental Health Movement

By Cho Ming Xiu, Founder & Executive Director,
Campus PSY Limited

Ming Xiu talks about the need to shift the culture of help-seeking behaviour. While awareness for mental health issues have increased significantly in the last five years, if the mindsets or attitudes towards people with mental health conditions do not change, then no matter how many campaigns are run, we'll still experience pervasive stigmas in society.

STARTING AS A GROUND-UP INITIATIVE

MK

Tell me more about what you do with Campus PSY. What exactly inspired you to create that?

Ming Xiu

I'm the founder and executive director of Campus PSY. We're a youth mental health non-profit organization. We have four main pillars under us: advocacy, training, support, and volunteering. Next year, we will be going into interventions, providing intervention services like emotional support and counselling.

Over the years, we have been very blessed to have evolved from a ground-up initiative to a registered non-profit and are now moving towards a social service agency. Next year, we will be partnering with one of the public healthcare agencies for a new mental health programme to provide outreach and basic emotional support services to the youths in Singapore. So we're quite excited for what is to come.

MINDSET AND ATTITUDES NEED TO CHANGE

MK

Nice. Now, because you work a lot with people on the ground level and even at the campaign level itself, what are some of the biggest stigmas that you observed about mental health?

Ming Xiu

Right so. Wah, that's quite a lot.

[Ming Xiu laughs]

MK

That's a heavy question, I know.

Ming Xiu

Over the years, we've worked with all these campaigns and outreach events, and we've also had focus group discussions and feedback from young people and their family members. A lot of young people have told us that they're very heartened that over the past five years, there's been a lot of nationwide mental-health-related stigmatization campaigns like Beyond the Label and ground-up initiatives that are sprouting up. But awareness is one thing. I think they are still fearful of seeking professional help. Their main concern is that for those on scholarship, if they share their medical history, they might not be able to get the scholarships or even get into the universities that they want. And it's the same for young working adults. They're also fearful that if they disclose this with HR, they might not be able to get the job that they want. But the thing is, as you know, the Ministry of Manpower—I think since last year, they've removed the clause requiring people to disclose their mental health condition unless they want to share it. I think that's one step closer in ensuring young Singaporeans that it is okay that if you have a past medical history or psychiatric history, that if you are willing to work in recovery, then the workplace, your employers, or even institutions will support you in your journey itself.

The other thing is the treatment gap, defined as the period of time between the moment the person suspects that he or she has a mental health condition or is diagnosed with that, and the moment they go and seek help. In Singapore, the treatment gap is pretty long. If you go and look up the Singapore Mental Health Study 2016[53],

---

[53] Subramaniam, M., E. Abdin, J. A. Vaingankar, S. Shafie, B. Y. Chua, R. Sambasivam, Y. J. Zhang, et al., 'Tracking the Mental Health of a Nation: Prevalence and Correlates of Mental Disorders in the Second Singapore Mental

it's usually a few years before people go and seek professional help. And also, the feedback, not just from young Singaporeans but also Singaporeans in general, is that the waiting time is pretty long if they want to go to public hospitals or even polyclinics to arrange for an appointment with a psychiatrist or psychologist.

Accessibility wise, there's a disparity in terms of the cost. In public hospitals and polyclinics, you pay a subsidized rate because the government actually subsidizes your treatment. But if you go to private GPs or even private psychiatrists or psychologists, an hour of therapy might easily cost you about $100+ to $200, so to a young person who's still studying, or working, or just started working, financially it's quite heavy lah, for them. Then of course, this serves as a deterrent to seeking help. But the thing is, people are more inclined to go towards private practice, because the records won't be on public domains. But it's also more expensive, so there are a lot of concerns with regards to accessibility, affordability and confidentiality.

MK

Got it. And how do you think we are able to overcome this? How do you think we can intervene from an individual, to a collective, and a governmental level so that we can overcome or reduce all these forces that are stopping people from seeking help?

Ming Xiu

I think what needs to shift is really the culture around help-seeking behaviour. There's a lot of awareness out there on a national level and from different agencies. But the thing is that if the mindsets or attitudes of Singaporeans towards people with mental health conditions don't change, meaning that they still stigmatize people who are struggling with mental health conditions, then no matter

---

Health Study', Epidemiology and Psychiatric Sciences 29, 2020: e29. doi:10.1017/S2045796019000179

how many campaigns you run, people will still know that in reality, that's not the case. So systemically, what employers and schools can do is to be a role model. I think that bosses can share about their personal struggles to reassure employees that it is okay to go and seek professional help because they themselves, as bosses or supervisors, have been through it, and this will help to build trust among Singaporeans. Schools, teachers, and educators, or even course instructors, can also share their challenges or provide resources that students can go to and reassure them that it will not impede their academic progression in terms of their scholarship applications or their future post-graduate studies. I think this sort of assurance from schools and workplaces will help quite a bit in terms of building trust among Singaporeans to go and seek help.

Trust is a key factor here. A shift in mindset and role modelling systemically. I think nationally, we're progressing.

As you can see, there are different inter-agency task forces like the Youth Mental Wellbeing Network led by the government, and the different agencies are also coming together to do more. But like I said, beyond awareness and campaigns, we will need to work more closely with the ground, with the schools and workplaces, to actualize the destigmatization efforts and make it a reality so that people will believe in it.

I think what individuals can do as friends or family members, colleagues, or classmates, is to train ourselves to be first responders or peer supporters with basic mental health knowledge or skills so that they can be the first line of support or network of defence. Because usually, if a person is struggling with a mental health condition, the first people they go to are their friends. And this is backed by research. The Ministry of Education is going to do so by 2021—they're looking to train all students in primary and secondary schools and even junior colleges during CCE[54] in very basic mental health knowledge so

[54] CCE: Character and Citizenship Education

that they will be able to identify certain signs of mental health conditions for their friends.

As friends and family, we can be more empathetic instead of being dismissive. I think what we learn is that active listening really helps. So really being present, being there, and not be judgemental towards what the person is sharing with you or whether the person is diagnosed with a mental health condition, just listening to their challenges and their struggles and assuring them that there are people around them who love and care for them, showing them unconditional love—these will really help. You know the starfish story? If one person throws one starfish back into the sea, then we can save one starfish. So if one person can be trained to listen to someone, this creates a ripple effect, and slowly, that will multiply. When people say they have a flu or physical condition like diabetes, they will just go and see a GP or a doctor and they won't be stigmatized for it. My dream is that, not just in Singapore, but in the world, when people say they think they are in distress or they might be struggling with depression or anxiety or different mental health conditions, they're not afraid that people will judge. Or, when they want to share their vulnerability, that there will be people who are equipped with the relevant knowledge and skill sets to support them. That's my vision for Singapore.

MK

Excellent, excellent, excellent! Wow.
[Ming Xiu laughs]

DISCONNECT TO CONNECT

MK

Those things that you're sharing, you know, it is out there, but yet it's so invisible to people. We can't assume that all this general knowledge is actually common knowledge. So I find this whole conversation very informative. Now, Ming Xiu, I'm going to ask you one last question: if you had a final message to the world about how we can change the mental health scape, what would that be?

Ming Xiu

I think my message is . . .

So you know that in Singapore, based on the NCSS[55] studies right, one in seven Singaporeans are struggling with mental health conditions, and that will actually increase over the next few years. And in fact, for young people, it's one in five. So that's about twenty per cent and that's underreported. So can you imagine? Even the World Health Organization says that the COVID-19 situation exacerbated the mental health epidemic because more people are isolated in their homes, and that exacerbates the different mental health conditions. I think there are a lot of things people can do. Not sure if you watched The Social Dilemma, but what people can do, what the world can do, is disconnect to connect. Yeah. I think that's a message I hope to end off with. Your initiative is called ThisConnect, right?

MK

Yes, and you know what's the most coincidental thing? I just had a conversation with one of the Ministers a couple of hours ago and this was the message that I ended up with: Disconnect to connect. This was the exact same message that I ended up with just two hours ago!

Ming Xiu

Oh great, great! Awesome. So my message is really disconnect to connect because in this world that we're living in, we're constantly

---

[55] NCSS: National Council of Social Service

on our phones, on the different social media platforms to seek validation. That's especially true for the younger ones, right? Because they're born in this tech era. So the thing is, research has also shown that it has exacerbated the mental health epidemic because we have lost the connections that we forge when we go out there and connect with our friends face to face or even create communities. And we've forgotten to connect as a community to support one another. So if the world can start to take some time off social media to disconnect and to connect more physically and to be present, be there when someone needs a listening ear and be that listening ear, I think the world would be a better place. There would be less people who are distressed and more people who are more loving and empathetic towards one another.

And there's another thing. So I think the connect to disconnect, disconnect to connect is really about the different distractions. Recently on YouTube, I watched this book review called Making Time and it says there are two types of distractions. One is the busy bandwagon and the other one is all your tech-related distractions. The busy bandwagon is where currently everyone feels that as long as you're busy, you're being productive, which means that you're living a very fulfilled life.
[Ming Xiu laughs]

Whether you are busy in your career, in school, or whatever you're busy with, people wear it like a badge of honour—but really, does being busy also translate to having a productive life, a joyful life, or a fulfilled life? I think that's what we need to shift in terms of the narrative of success or the narrative of living a productive or busy life, instead of just hopping onto the bandwagon of being busy. I think it's especially difficult for Singaporeans because we pride ourselves as the hub for so many things! (laughing) The hub for the banking and finance industry, and we're also going to be the tech hub soon, so I think it's top down. It's a very systemic kind of thing but it's also because Singapore thrives on that—our survival depends on competition and achievements. But if you really want to protect the mental wellbeing of our citizens, then I think we need to relook at how we can protect our young people from this busy bandwagon and the different distractions from social media to help them live more authentic lives.

CHAPTER 15

You Don't Need To Be A Therapist To Be Therapeutic

By Asher Low, Executive Director, Limitless

There is an increasing number of youths reaching out for mental health care, and that number rose sharply during the height of the Covid-19 pandemic. Asher shared that for youths, sometimes the people who stigmatise against their conditions are their parents, church leaders, principals, and these stigmas are what make intervention work much more difficult. Social support is extremely important, because the reality is that many people resolve their issues not just because they see a therapist, but also because they have a support system walking alongside them.

LIKE A TREE BRANCH SNAPPING

Asher

I'm a social worker by training. When we started Limitless, it was to reach out to all youths out there—the disenfranchised, the *ah beng*[56], the *ah lian*[57]. But when we opened our doors for clients to come in, for youths to seek help, we realized that almost every single youth that walked through our doors within the first few months came in for mental health issues. We realized that there was a huge need, because if they're coming to us, it probably means that they have nowhere else to go. And we realized that that was the need at the moment, so we pivoted our direction and we went into mental health. And ever since then, the numbers have just been growing, year on year, especially last year when we saw a thirty per cent increase, and we're expecting that same level of increase this year as well because of the current situation. So that was that. I didn't get into this because I wanted to. I got into this because the need was there.

MK

What made you decide to want to become a social worker?

Asher

I've always wanted to work with youths. I was working with youths for more than ten years before I became a social worker. So while I was doing that, I got my degree, went into family work, went into prison work, and I think the key thing that I always wanted to do was to work with young people, and it just so happens that

---

[56] Ah beng: A stereotype applied to a teenage or twenty-something Chinese male in Singapore who acts like a gangster

[57] Ah lian: A stereotype applied to a teenage or twenty-something Chinese female in Singapore who acts like a gangster

I'm still doing that. Just not in the context that I ever dreamed I would be doing it.

MK

Would you mind sharing about the mental health issues youths face today?

Asher

What I realize is that very often, the struggles come about because of a few things: family, trauma, and relationships in school. These are the three most common things that we see, and to be honest, the most challenging types of cases that we see are those whose issues stem from family. Because they're youths, they're underaged, and they're still in the same home as their parents, they're in that very unconducive environment for recovery. Those are the most challenging because the reality is that if a family member is contributing to the mental health issue, it's most likely that they're not willing to make any changes to help that young person recover from that mental health issue.

Every young person is different. They respond differently to therapy, they respond differently to the challenges in their lives, so some of them might come in with very major issues but it stems from a minor situation. It didn't start as a very major or a very *jialat*[58] traumatic experience. But someone else might come in with the same or similar experience, and is coping and dealing with it very well. So the differences are quite real there.

MK

Got it. And what are the mental health trends among Singapore youths today?

---

[58] Jialat: Singapore slang that describes a dire situation

Asher

More people are struggling. I think the reality is that COVID-19 has played a huge role in affecting our mental health.

The thing is that when things are out of control, it generally affects our mental wellbeing. And when we are in such an unpredictable situation—in this case, the pandemic—the consistent changes affect our ability to respond and cope. There were several major disruptions and changes for youths to cope with since COVID-19. We went into lockdown. They had to adapt to virtual classes, couldn't hang out with their friends anymore, and worried that their dad's company may have to close down—and these changes and uncertainties are happening all at the same time. That consistent level of stress creates a burden that is more than what a lot of people are able to handle on their own.

If you think about it from the perspective of us as a tree branch, basically what's happening is that more and more things are being piled on top of that branch, and eventually the branch will break because of the amount of weight on it. That's the situation that we're in right now. Whether you come from a better socioeconomic status, or a worse one, the reality is that because of all these stresses to our social, emotional, economic, even the physical areas in our lives, it's become very challenging for people to manage. And when that happens, that's when mental health goes downhill.

And what we saw in the previous year was a huge increase in young people seeking help for trauma-related issues. And unsurprisingly, the cases that we had existing at that point in time all started to deteriorate and get more serious. We had cases that were code green, meaning that they were stable, they were coping well, but within a few months or even weeks after the Circuit Breaker[59], they started to go red. We had cases that were

---

[59] Circuit Breaker refers to the three-month nationwide lockdown in Singapore to curb the spread of COVID-19

red, and unfortunately, one of our youths took her life during the Circuit Breaker. I think the reality is that being in that hyper-stressful situation can cause mental health to go downhill, and that's something that we're going to see moving forward.

IF YOU HAVE FOOD POISONING FOR SIX YEARS, YOU TRY LAH!

MK

What was the biggest stigma that you faced when dealing with your mental health?

Asher

When we are advocating for people with mental health issues, there will always be people who stigmatise them. Sometimes those people come in the form of parents. Sometimes they come in the form of church leaders. Sometimes they come in the form of school principals. The challenge is that if they play such a key role in this young person's life and they have stigmas against that young person, that's when we find that our work becomes way, way, way harder.

When I grew up with my own mental health issues, I never told anyone because back then, the stigma was very real. And in my own life, there was also a lot of self-stigma like *it can't be me, can't be something is wrong with me,* that kind of issue. But at the end of the day when I was struggling with my own head space, I felt that I shouldn't tell anyone. And that was the challenge then. But now, it's much easier. I can tell my friends, or a young person can tell his or her friends and the people of that same generation, chances are, most likely they will give support. It's very interesting.

MK

What was causing the self-stigma for you back then?

Asher

I think the challenge for myself back then was the fear that people would think there's something wrong with me and that I was going to lose opportunities in life—I was going to lose the opportunity to be the class leader, the CCA leader. I was going to lose my opportunity to serve in church, that kind of thing. That was the major challenge that I had because of the perception that people had of those around me who struggled with mental health issues.

When you're afraid that you'll lose your social standing, when you're afraid that you'll lose your social support system, I think that's when stigma becomes very real, and that's the reason why many young people don't seek help, actually. If we look at the statistics, one-third to two-thirds of young people will not seek help if they're struggling with their mental health issues. And when they do, it usually takes them up to six years, statistically. So imagine having stomach ache for six years before you finally go to the doctor—doesn't make sense to me lah!
[laughter]

Asher

But you know, I like to use the example of poisoning actually. If you have food poisoning for six years, you try lah!
[laughter]

Asher

And if we look at the statistics internationally—we don't know local statistics because we don't have them yet—about fifty per cent of people diagnosed with mental health issues start to see symptoms by the age of fourteen, and seventy-five per cent of them start to see them by the age of twenty-five. So, that's a lot of people, young people! If I'm fourteen and I'm struggling with thoughts that *I'm lousy* and I'm struggling with an uncontrollable and unexplainable sadness, by the time I reach twenty and I finally seek help, very often, those issues have evolved into way worse things. And that's the challenge we are seeing.

But I think that the good thing about this generation is that they're more woke lah. They're supportive of one another. They're able to tell each other, 'Hey, you're struggling, let's go see someone'. 'Hey, you're struggling, let me help you'. 'Hey, you're struggling, you ok? Can I send you a froyo?'
[laughter]

Asher

And that's when social support comes in. And the reality is that for anyone who struggles with things like mood or anxiety issues, a lot of them resolve that issue without having to see a doctor, counsellor, therapist, or social worker, and very often we can attribute a large part of that to the support system the young person has. And that was the same for me as well. I only started seeing someone when I was in my twenties, but I struggled with my issues since I was in my teens. But because I knew I had a support system that I could go to talk to about every other thing besides mental health, and that helped me recover as well. On top of that, it was my own faith that helped me through my own troubles as well. So when we look at young people today, I have hope that they're in a much better space than I was when I was sixteen.

YOU'VE FOUGHT A GOOD BATTLE AND WON

MK

Got it. How do you think we can overcome stigmas, whether it is from an individual or a collective level?

Asher

The best way to deal with stigma is to talk about it until it becomes normal. So I always say this—my hope is that one day, Singapore can be like people in Australia and the US, where I can tell my friend 'I can't meet you for lunch, I'm going to see my therapist', and the response is not *oh my god* and immediate judgement, but instead is 'Eh, your therapist good or not? Do you think I should go too? Can you give me a recommendation?' I think that's when the stigma ends. But we've not reached that point yet. I hope that in a couple of years, we do.

But when we talk about it, when you make it part of your daily life, that stigma disappears and goes away. And the way to deal with it is to talk about it like it's a normal medical condition and treat people who have struggled and recovered from mental health issues the same way we treat people who have struggled and recovered from cancer. We treat them like heroes. I think we should do the same for mental health. There's this whole belief that people with mental health issues are weak, especially from the older generations. It's a suck it up, deal with it, kind of mentality that a lot of them have. But the reality is that for someone who can deal with an issue for six, seven, eight years, that is, in certain ways, just as debilitating as a physical condition like cancer, just as painful, and takes more lives—if we can treat them the same way we treat someone who's recovering from cancer, like they've fought a good battle and won, I think the stigma would go.

MK

Any last food for thought that you want to leave people with?

Asher

Food for thought . . . I think the biggest food for thought would be that I recovered from my mental health issues because of the support that I had. You never know how much your genuine care and love and support can help someone else along the way. Whether you suspect something or you don't suspect something, just be a good friend and family member. I think that in and of itself is recovery. And I often say this when I run training sessions and I speak to leaders and parents and all of that: 'You don't have to be a therapist to be therapeutic'. The recovery often happens in relationships. And of course, sometimes there's a need for medication. Sometimes there's a need for a therapist to step in. But very often, recovery happens in relationships. So that's food for thought.

CHAPTER 16

Where Are You In The Picture?

By Natalie Kang, MA AThR,
Registered Art Psychotherapist,
MySpace Psychotherapy Services, Art For Good

Having worked with diverse groups of people, Natalie shares the different ways stigma manifests in society. And oftentimes, people with mental health conditions have to deal with the cultural stigmas that come with it. For instance, the belief that having a mental health condition is the result of bad karma from wrongdoing in a past life. At the end of the day, we have to stop, listen to ourselves, and ask how we experience it for ourselves, how we truly feel about it, instead of feeding and listening to the voices of those around us at the expense of ourselves.

FINDING RESONANCE

MK

What got you interested in mental health issues?

Natalie

I had many personal encounters. The most significant was losing a friend to bipolar disorder when I was fourteen. That left a huge impact on me. At that point in time, I didn't understand anything about bipolar disorder, depression, and mental health issues. As I grew older, I became curious about why people behave the way they did, and realized that my friend was suffering from a mental health condition. That was about fifteen years back, when it was still a very taboo conversation and topic—especially for me at that age. Nobody spoke to me about it, or sat me down to explain and say 'You know what, she was actually experiencing this, this, and this, so therefore it led to certain behaviours'. It was not widely discussed or shared about, but I believe that incident sowed a seed in me and from that point onwards, I started becoming interested in mental-health-related issues and special needs.

MK

Heavy stuff.

Many people still don't really understand what art therapy is about. What do people need to know about art therapy, and how art can help where mental health issues are concerned?

Natalie

Art therapy is a combination of arts and psychology, where we use psychological concepts coupled with artmaking to support the individual in their own process of discovery. We look at the whole person and create a safe space and provide containment for them to process the thoughts and emotions that come up through their art. Art therapists also employ arts-based assessments to gain insight and understanding of their clients through their artwork. While I encourage free expression within the session, there are also times when I will give or share certain art directives or themes with my clients. For instance, I may encourage clients to work with clay or create a worry doll.

In my work with youths living with mental health conditions, they have shared many times that the process of art making in art therapy is helpful in reducing their stress levels, in teasing out certain emotions, so they can be clearer about their own emotions that otherwise feel jumbled together and messy inside. At times, they find it confrontational too when they gain an awareness of some of the strong and intense emotions within, and it's challenging for them to face it. The use of art—from splashing paints to throwing clay—then helps them to explore, express, contain, and process these emotions within. This is also where cathartic release comes into play. This helps them to sublimate some of their negative impulses and urges such as self-harming through the process of art-making. The use of different mediums also evokes different feelings and reactions within the youths, and it's something that I look out for.

But of course, it's not always that easy. You don't go in and say 'Here's a piece of clay, would you like to throw it?' No. It's a process, and it often starts with building a strong therapeutic relationship with the client, and giving them a sense of safety and security.

YOU BROUGHT IT UPON YOURSELF

MK

I know that you work with diverse groups of people. What is something about them that perhaps the public has misunderstood or lacks awareness in?

Natalie

It really depends—it's a very diverse group as you mentioned. Children with mental health conditions or special needs and their caregivers is one population, and adolescents or youths at-risk is another.

For at-risk youths, many have been labelled by society as bad apples. They have been labelled as, 自找的， meaning that they brought it upon themselves. And it's really painful to hear that because almost all the at-risk youths that I've met have had some form of challenging family background, or they've experienced some form of bullying or adverse situation that shaped them into who they are today. And to say that they brought it upon themselves, serves them right—I think it's unfair and unhelpful towards them and their recovery process as a whole. Those with mental health conditions often adopt the narrative that *I'm crazy, I'm locked up here, nobody understands or loves me*—these things come up in my work with them and their descriptions of themselves.

MK

Very defeating conversations.

Natalie

Yes, there's a lot of defeating conversations surrounding these youths.

On the other hand, for children living with special needs and mental health conditions, a lot of stress is upon their caregivers. Amongst the older generation, there seems to be this prevailing stigma that their caregivers or parents must have done something wrong. I often hear comments such as, 他们上一辈子没积德，所以这一辈子轮到孩子 *(they didn't accumulate good deeds in their past life, so it's on their children now)*. Some caregivers do beat themselves up. They feel guilty about giving birth to a child with special needs, even though we know that it's hereditary, and I've had parents who shared their shame and guilt with me, and this makes it challenging to celebrate their child. The public's sentiment and acceptance also seem to be negative and lacking—I've heard recounts of parents with children living with ASD[60] that their greatest fear when bringing their child out is to navigate through a meltdown in public. They shared about the stares that burn through them and it pushes them into this frenzy to calm or control or do all they can to make the child keep quiet so that they can reduce the staring. And we do see this occurring at times when a kid shouts or throws a tantrum in public. These stares seem to make parents feel further ashamed and alienated, which isn't helpful because it adds to the stress that they are already experiencing . . .

MK

. . . There are too many stigmas around it.

HOW OFTEN DO YOU LISTEN TO YOURSELF?

MK

What are some of the assumptions, misconceptions or unrealistic expectations that people actually have about the mental health treatment process?

Natalie

I think some of them think we're miracle workers. I always emphasize that it's a process, but you have to learn to trust the process at the same time. I understand and fully empathize with the parents, especially with their anxiety over their child. But I have parents who, after one or two sessions, come in and ask, 'Hey, my

---

[60] ASD: Autism Spectrum Disorder

kid's still the same! Why is it not working?' And I then have to explain to them how it is a process for some children. Some require long-term therapy and support that can last up to six months or a year. For some children, you may see improvement within a short amount of time. It really depends as no two individuals are the same. The same goes for the mental health treatment process—it's hardly one-size-fits-all. But of course, I do have children whose parents came back after two sessions and happily shared about the change they saw—about how their child was sharing and opening up more, and how therapy supported and aided in rebuilding and strengthening their parent-child relationship.

I believe everyone needs to work hand in hand during the treatment process. This includes parents, caregivers, the environment at home, in school, or at work, and collaborating with the therapist and engaging in the therapy sessions. But at times, when parents or caregivers are fatigued themselves, this can be challenging. They have to juggle all their responsibilities at work and at home on top of caring for their child with needs.

MK

Definitely, it's all on them.

Natalie

And it doesn't help when they come in and say 'Oh my friends say this, my relatives say that, my grandparents say this, everyone says this' and I'm like

MK

Then where's the truth?

Natalie

Yeah, and so at times I'll ask 'How do you experience it for yourself? What about you? What do you say? How do you feel?'

Where is the *you* in it, you know? Sometimes all these voices come in, and it covers up their own voice and their own hopes and dreams for the child. And I ask them 'What about your child? What is he or she saying?'

Some parents come in fully exasperated like 'I don't know how, I don't know what I can do anymore', and I've come to realize that it's important to meet the parents at where they are, in the here and now. I have come to realize that in my work with children and adolescents, I have to support the parents as well. It's a package.

MK

How do you think people can support their loved ones more effectively through their mental health struggles?

Natalie

Provide a listening ear. They may come to you with the same problem repeatedly, but one thing you can always do is to listen and affirm them. I think the most common response when these problems get repeated, is 'Huh, why is it still the same problem? Didn't I tell you the answer already? Haven't you grown out of this? Just last week you were telling me about the same thing'. But it's important for us to listen without any judgement, and paraphrase or acknowledge what they say and their feelings, and also to hold our comments to ourselves. I find that at times, we are so trained as a society to be solution-focused—but that might not be the most helpful thing in this context.

MK

It's as though these solutions we come up with are one-size-fits-all.

Natalie

Sometimes when you can withhold your solutions or opinions, you may be surprised that the other party may come up with their own solutions. While some may require support in brainstorming their next steps, oftentimes, it's not that they don't know what they need to do—it's just that it's so challenging for them to do it right now.

I understand too that some people offer solutions as they feel helpless seeing their loved one suffer. If you really want to do something, perhaps you can ask, 'Is there anything I can do, just to make your day a little bit better? Would you like a warm cup of tea or your favourite drink? Can I spend time with you? Can I watch your favourite show together with you?' What can I do with you? Little things like this go a long way.

THE RIPPLE EFFECT

MK

I know we're running out of time for this interview, but I think this question is important. How do you think we can reduce the stigma around mental health?

Natalie

I believe in the ripple effect, that one person at a time, word and awareness will spread. I'm honestly heartened to see more campaigns, and more organizations and workplaces starting to talk about mental health and wellness, self-care, and taking steps to educate their employees or the public. I believe it will pave the way to a more inclusive society; towards a society that has greater tolerance, awareness, and acceptance of mental health issues.

MK

Thank you! That was very extensive. I loved it.

Natalie

I hope too that we can see a different Singapore five or ten years later. How do we envision the mental health scene to develop? I think that's something we also have to think about and ask fellow mental health professionals or advocates in this field. How would things be five or ten years down the road? Of course, I hope that it's for the better.

The path to finding the answers is not easy by any means, and sometimes the answers aren't what we expect them to be. But there are 1001 reasons not to do something, and you only need one to do it—because **your life matters.** Doors and windows of opportunity open when they do, and it is up to you to step in. If the experience of this book has sparked something deeper in you that you wish to examine, let this be another sign from the universe to keep going.

If you'd like to reach out to have a conversation with us, our doors are open.

Send us a message on Instagram at **@thisconnect.today,** and we'll be happy to connect with you.

Bibliography

Chu, Chi Meng, Thomas, Stuart D. M., and Ng, Vivienne, 'Childhood Abuse And Delinquency: A Descriptive Study Of Institutionalized Female Youth In Singapore.' *Psychiatry, Psychology And Law*, 2009, 16 (sup1): S64-S73. doi:10.1080/13218710802552971.

Herzog, Julia I., and Schmahl, Christian, 'Adverse Childhood Experiences And The Consequences On Neurobiological, Psychosocial, And Somatic Conditions Across The Lifespan.' *Front Psychiatry*, 2019, 9:420. doi:10.3389/fpsyt.2018.00420.

Kim Ho, 'A Third Of Singaporeans Have Experienced Suicidal Thoughts.' *Yougov: What The World Thinks*, 2019, https://sg.yougov.com/en-sg/news/2019/06/25/sg-mentalhealth-selfharm/

Liu, Denise, Chu, Chi Meng, Lee, Hong Neo, Ang, Rebecca P.,Tan, Michelle, and Chu, Jeanie, 'Multiple Trauma Exposure And Psychosocial Functioning In Singaporean Children In Out-Of-Home Care.' *Psychological Trauma: Theory, Research, Practice, And Policy*, 2016, 8 (4): 431-438. doi:10.1037/tra0000098

Subramaniam, M., E. Abdin, J. A. Vaingankar, S. Shafie, B. Y. Chua, R. Sambasivam, Y. J. Zhang, et al., 'Tracking the Mental Health of a Nation: Prevalence and Correlates of Mental Disorders in the Second Singapore Mental Health

Study.' *Epidemiology and Psychiatric Sciences* 29, 2020: e29. doi:10.1017/S2045796019000179.

Toh, Sze Min, Fu, Charlene, Chan, Qing Rong, Fang, Xinwei, and Nisa Nurdini Binte Johar, 'Do Close Relationships with Caregivers Help Build Children's Resilience to Adversity?' *Research Bites*, 2019, https://www.childrensociety.org.sg/resources/ck/files/research-bites-issue-8-february-2020.pdf

Yeager, David S., and Dweck, Carol S., 'Mindsets That Promote Resilience: When Students Believe That Personal Characteristics Can Be Developed.' *Educational Psychologist,* 2012, 47 (4): 302-314. doi:10.1080/00461520.2012.722805.

Acknowledgements

I would like to express our heartfelt gratitude to all the people who have played a part in making this book come to life. To our contributors, thank you for jumping in and contributing your time, energy, and intention towards forwarding the mental health scene in Singapore. It is a work in progress, and perhaps it may take more than just one lifetime to see the transformation unfold, yet your desire to make a difference to the people out there is instrumental to keeping the vision alive for our future generations, in wellness and prosperity. I am grateful to all of you for the good work that is being done out there and I look forward to more efficient and effective interventions to touch the lives out there.

To the people working with me in the background, Si Qi and Megan, I want to thank you for supporting me in facilitating the process so that these interviews and the backend work could happen. Your beliefs in the cause and my vision, your stand, dedication, and devotion in the project have inspired me to keep going, to push forth to produce a higher quality of work that is nothing less than being impeccable and excellent. This book would not have been completed without your support and commitment.

We embarked on this project with the simple objective to document the different perspectives around mental health in Singapore, yet we walked out of each interview session feeling deeply inspired by selfless acts of service from all these contributors. These interview sessions have shaped our understanding of what service to the community means, no matter big or small, and we deeply cherish the life lessons and personal takeaways we received from all the contributors.

I would also like to attribute and honor all my masters and teachers for being my greatest sources of inspiration for my work, and the trust and faith they placed in me in carrying the work forward to make a difference in this world; trusting in me to do the right thing and getting my act together during my lowest point and being there with me to celebrate my successes and endeavors during my highest peaks. Without them, I would not have been the person I am today. Every single day, I wake up looking forward to live my mark with love, passion and joy.

Finally, I would like to conclude with a quote from Thoreau, Henry David Thoreau, *Walden, or Life in the Woods*:

'I went to the woods because I wished to live deliberately, to front only the essential facts of life, and see if I could not learn what it had to teach, and not, when I came to die, discover that I had not lived. I did not wish to live what was not life, living is so dear; nor did I wish to practice resignation, unless it was quite necessary. I wanted to live deep and suck out all the marrow of life, to live so sturdily and Spartan-like as to put to rout all that was not life, to cut a broad swath and shave close, to drive life into a corner, and reduce it to its lowest terms, and, if it proved to be mean, why then to get the whole and genuine meanness of it, and publish its meanness to the world; or if it were sublime, to know it by experience, and be able to give a true account of it in my next excursion.'

This is an experience we will remember for a lifetime, and we hope that it has inspired you to continue doing the work that you do too. This is only the beginning, and there is so much more to learn, many more steps to take, and much more work to be done.

We hope to honour all our contributors by doing our part to champion mental health causes so that we can create an inclusive, thriving society where people are deeply connected to themselves, to the present, and to the world around them. Thank you.

Acknowledgements

Adrian Pang
Pangdemonium

Amirah Munawwarah
ImPossible Psychological Services

Andrea Chan
Joel Wong
Lucia Chow
Peggy Lim
TOUCH Community Services Ltd

Asher Low
Limitless

Belinda Ang
ARTO by thinkART of the Box Pte Ltd

Brenda Lee
Lynn Tan
The Psychology Practice

Buvenasvari Pragasam
Solace Art Psychotherapy Pte Ltd

Camellia Wong
InPsychful LLP

Carrie Tan
Nee Soon South (Nee Soon GRC)

Calvin Eng
Association for Music Therapy (Singapore)

Charlotte Goh
Playeum

Cheryl Chan
Fengshan (East Coast GRC)

Cayden Woo
Jeremy Heng
Singapore Children's Society

Cho Ming Xiu
Campus PSY Limited

Daphne Chua
Somatic Therapy Asia

David Chew
National Heritage Board

David Lim
Tzu Chi Free Clinic
Special Oral Care Network

Deborah Seah
Nadera Binte Abdul Aziz
Community of
Peer Support
Specialists (CPSS)

Desmond Chew
Jacqueline
Jamie
Mysara
Caregivers Alliance Limited

Desmond Soh
Annabelle Psychology

Eric Chua
Ministry of Culture,
Community and Youth
Ministry of Social and
Family Development

Etsegenet Mulugeta Eshete
Margaret Hoffer
Selamta Family Project

Goh Li Shan
REACH (West)
Department of
Psychological Medicine,
National University
Hospital

Hannah Batrisyia
Muhammad Syazan
Bin Saad
Temasek Polytechnic

Jamus Lim
Anchorvale
(Sengkang GRC)

Jasmine Yeo
The Private Practice

Jenny Ng
Conscious Parenting Coach
(MEd of Family Education)

Jingzhou
Cassia Resettlement Team

Josephine Chia-Teo
InSightful Training &
Consultancy Pte Ltd

John Wong Chee Meng
Department of Psychological Medicine, National University Hospital

Jun Lee
Self-employed Art Therapist and Art Facilitator

Karen Wee
Lions Befrienders Service Association

Kyl Lim
Singapore Cancer Society

Lynette Har
ICF-Certified Peak Performance Coach

Lynette Seow
Safe Space™

Marion Neubronner
Psychologist and Leadership Development Coach

Michelle Koay
St. Joseph's Institution International Ltd

Murali Pillai
Bukit Batok SMC

Narasimman S/O Tivasiha Mani
Impart Ltd

Navin Amarasuriya
The Contentment Foundation

Natalie Kang
Art for Good Pte Ltd
MySpace Psychotherapy Services Pte Ltd

Nicole K.
The Tapestry Project SG

Jolene
Volunteer in the Migrant Worker Space

Nur Farhan Bte Mohammad Alami
Raffles Medical Group

Ng Gim Choo
The EtonHouse Group

Ng Jek Mui
Dementia Singapore (formerly known as Alzheimer's Disease Association)

Patrick Tay
Pioneer SMC

Rachel Yang
Daylight Creative Therapies

Ronald P.M.H. Lay
LASALLE College of the Arts

Roshni Bhatia
Yoko Choi
FoundSpace

Seah Kian Peng
Braddell Heights (Marine Parade GRC)

Serene Seng
Senserene Pte Ltd

Siew Kum Yew
Shan You Counselling Centre

Simone Heng
Human Connection Speaker

Sun Kaiying
Hope for Tomorrow Psychology Centre

Sufian Yusof
Aileron Wellness

Tina Hung
National Council of Social Service (NCSS)

Tin Pei Ling
MacPherson SMC

Wan Rizal Bin Wan Zakariah
Kolam Ayer (Jalan Besar GRC)

Vickineswarie Jagadharan
OTHERS

Victor Mills
Michael Chang
Sujata Tiwari
Singapore International Chamber of Commerce

Ying Jie

About THISCONNECT.TODAY

THIS
. CON
NECT

ThisConnect is a mental health advocacy community set up to spark more conscious awareness and forwarding interventions on mental health, emotional wellness, and suicide prevention using experiential art. We recognise the need to begin the mental health conversations by examining the personal struggles that weigh us down in life. These everyday stressors can seem insignificant on their own, but over a long period of time, they can make us feel trapped, lost, stressed, and depressed. Through our work, we want to inspire more people to step out, to connect consciously and deeply with themselves physically, emotionally, mentally and spiritually, and to find the healing with the good and the bad, the positive and the negative, the light and the shadow within them. We want people to access their courage, love, freedom in their beings to express their most authentic selves, and to create a life where they are thriving. We hope that our work will empower individuals to seek help and to look inwards whenever they face challenges in life.

Since 2020, we have presented three large multimedia art exhibitions and thirteen moving satellite shows in Singapore, titled *ThisConnect: Threading Worlds*, Masks of Singapore, and *ThisConnect: What Am I, If I Am Not*, and were featured in *The Straits Times*,

Tatler, Channel 8. Masks of Singapore, a six-month community participatory art project movement, has set the record for the 'Largest Mosaic of Hand-Sculptured Masks' in the Singapore Book of Records and were documented into a photobook with Fujifilm that tells 572 lived-stories of individuals from all walks of lives in their most authentic self behind the masks created.

For more information, reach out at

ThisConnect.today@gmail.com.
https://www.thisconnect.today
https://www.instagram.com/thisconnect.today

'Oftentimes, external expectations about who we should be and how we should act prevent us from being free to express ourselves and do the things that truly matter to us. As a result, many of us end up chasing after societal definitions of success instead of what truly matters to us, and we end up lost, confused, and disconnected from ourselves. It is this disconnection from ourselves that forms the start of the many mental and emotional struggles we face every day, and it is potentially leads to depression, and on a more severe scale, suicide. Through our work, we aim to explore the deeper conversations that underpin the mental health struggles many of us battle in our daily lives and empower people to connect to themselves, to the present, and the world around them. Ultimately, the goal is to see a society where people are free to be bold, be free, and be themselves—unapologetically—so that they can begin to live a life that matters to them.'

Hun Ming Kwang,
Founder, Creative Director,
Author of ThisConnect.today